Richard and Annette Rubin

Homescape Rewilding

Stories of Ordinary Ecological Practices

*The proceeds of this book will be
dedicated to organizations supporting
Rewilding ecology practices.*

ISBN: 978-1-7378109-0-2

Library of Congress Control Number: 2021945637

Cover photos, background image on chapter openers, and photograph on page xxv by Skip Belyea. All other photos courtesy of authors.

Book and cover design by Anne Flanagan (adfbooks@mac.com)

Published by Nighthawk Press, P.O. Box 1222, Taos, New Mexico. 87571.

www.nighthawkpress.com

Printed in the United States of America.

NIGHTHAWK PRESS
TAOS, NEW MEXICO

Contents

Foreword

Aldo Leopold famously wrote, "The modern dogma is comfort at all costs." He was recognizing how so many of us cherish ease and security and how fierce we can be about avoiding inconvenience, danger, and the unknown. Leopold would be astounded at how far some people have gone in building comfortable lives. For many, life has become the equivalent of living in a cocoon. Ensconced in houses and traveling in cars, many of us are immune from the elements. We buy our food from a grocery store, draw energy from a plug, and drink sanitized water. We flip switches to get warmer or cooler (staying at roughly 72 all year round) and turn darkness into light. Few of us know where our water comes from or where our trash ultimately ends up. Indeed, it is even hard to get lost these days as we locate ourselves on GPS.

Living in a cocoon is nothing to scoff at. It often feels good not being pushed this way or that as the world around us changes, and it is certainly nice not having to worry constantly about the unknown. In our globalized world, especially for the affluent, many of us can eat the same food, workout in the same kind of gyms, sleep in the same kind of beds, and simply live a monochromatic life no matter what terrain we happen to be on. Comfort provides security, ease, and predictability.

But comfort also comes with costs. To get comfortable we often push wildness out of our lives, and this is having tragic effects on our home, the Earth, and even on our souls. We are all familiar with the litany of environmental harms our efforts to control the Earth have produced. Climate change, freshwater scarcity, loss of biological diversity, chemical toxification … the list goes on and on. We are also aware of how insulated we have become from the more-than-human world and how such isolation robs us from feeling the full depth of what it means to be human. Many of us, however, are puzzled of how to pull the human foot off the gas pedal and regain a sense of sanity in a world in environmental and social existential spasm. We yearn for connection and want to be involved in planetary healing and yet don't know where to start or at least ache to explore more promising routes toward personal and political transformation.

The book you hold in your hand provides a trail map of sorts. It offers dispatches from the frontlines of eco-personal endeavors and experimentation. At its core, it demonstrates the promise of Rewilding. The Rubins show us what it means to stop putting our boot-print on everything we encounter and how to open ourselves to the breathing, swirling world around us. They embrace difference and teach us how to attune ourselves to the other critters and plants we live among and to the history and changing contours of the places we call home. Living in the shadow of El Salto in Arroyo Seco, just outside of Taos, New Mexico, Richard and Annette show us through their experiences with planting and tending trees, growing ecologically and socially meaningful vegetables, cooking with respect to local traditions, and encouraging bees, birds, snakes, coyotes, et al, plus beloved canine companions, to live out their lives with greater veracity and autonomy. The Rubins' guiding vision is health—of one's own mind and body, one's family and friends, and the planet as a whole—and such wellbeing flourishes as we enhance the wild qualities of the world around us and the worlds within us.

The environmental writer, Richard Louv, has written, "We cannot protect something we do not love, we cannot love what we do not know, and we cannot know what we do not see. And touch. And hear." Annette and Richard teach us how to see, touch, and hear in their homescape, and demonstrate the love and care that follow. They are committed to practicality and to applying the wisdom that surfaces as one wrestles with how best to be awake ecological citizens of a planetary abode.

The urge to comfort has sent wildness into retreat. Everywhere we look the ax of control is felling the unwieldy nature of things. We know in our bones, however, the limits of such hegemony. We are not only eradicating the lives of the more-than-human world, deepening racial and other forms of injustice, and fomenting planetary fragility, we are also eviscerating our own sense of self, community, and place or, what Aldo Leopold called the "land community." I am grateful to Richard and Annette for having the courage to use their own life as testing ground for walking us away from the precipice that, otherwise, would stand increasingly closer to our toes. The insights they have perceived, practices they have cultivated, and the openness of their actions provide inspiration for navigating these harrowing times.

No one has the answer to our ecological woes. Living lightly and with integrity on the Earth is a perennial challenge. We need steady voices like the Rubins to walk us out into fields of possibility. Their words prod us to open our own eyes, get our hands dirty, and, most importantly, feel and amplify the pulse of wildness as it courses through life. May the wisdom of Rewilding come to touch all our lives.

Paul Wapner, Ph.D.
Professor, Global Environmental Politics
School of International Service
American University

Introduction

Acts of creation are ordinarily reserved for gods and poets, but humbler folk may circumvent this restriction if they know how. To plant a pine, for example, one need to be neither god nor poet; one need only own a shovel.   Aldo Leopold, *A Sand County Almanac,* 1949.

The authors of these stories are pragmatic people. We try to be informed by multicultural history and science. With careers as physician and educator, we build on lifelong usefulness. I attribute influence to the Freemasons who helped the Presbyterians rebuild my 1774 high school after the War of 1812 burning by the British. The motto then became: "Towards a widening sphere of usefulness."

We do not confuse this with utilitarian exploitation of the natural world. Rather, we strive to be useful members serving the ecosphere community. We call this book a journal because it records what we have done and learned. This is not

✦ Homescape and Hearth

a research study, handbook compilation, or theoretical plan. Many of the stories have come to us because of our choices in life of what to try, read, join, attempt, play, craft, observe, study, and value.

Creative inspiration messages are plentiful where we live. Beginning to write this in early January, Richard's Taos News Taurus horoscope said "The Capricorn New Moon of next Tuesday supports you with its grounding, practical influence. This would be a perfect time to reassess your present position and to plan out your New Year with practical ideas."

This small book is a collection of thoughts and efforts to pursue useful wildness in homescape ecologic practices. A Googled definition of *homescape* revealed "a meaningful place that is familiar enough to call home but also exists within a living, breathing, changing environment and cultural landscape." We agree with Luke Plotica's article in the October, 2020, *Ecological Citizen*: "Politics is not enough: Individual actions and the limits of institutions." He advances three claims: first, that individual action is itself an important ecological practice; second, that such action is needed to counteract the passive, irresponsible, consumerist mindset common with institutional policies; and third, that individual experimentation with ecologically responsible action provides models of more sustainable ways of living.

We do not pretend to expertise, but at our senior ages, we have many experiences to share. As Mark Twain advised, we write about what we know. We try to be wildly meaningful with what we have where we are. I believe the wisdom that the truly wealthy value what they have. Or as I learned in psychiatry, mental competence includes knowing the limits of one's bounty. Yet we also allow ourselves the Zen experience of "unknowingness" to enhance consciousness, as we learned from Taos teacher Sean Murphy at our Unity services.

There are many excellent journals and books about ecological subjects, ranging from political polemics to rigorous naturalist science texts to insightful literature and poetry. We will not attempt a comprehensive review of these works. The book you hold is written for a more ordinary level of interest, which in some way is all of us no matter what else we have or do.

I observe that some environmental literature is motivated by fashion for trendy entertainment. I became perceptive about this view from friend Ramona Scholder in 1975 when we worked in a Santa Fe community mental health clinic. We had many conversations about human psychology over lunch. She told a story about her husband Fritz, a well-known Na-

Native Otter

tive American artist, who had just completed a painting called "Fancy Dancer." Ramona said that more than the engaging colorful costume, he intended us to see the thin veneer of decoration.

But I do not denigrate all art in our community experience of wildness. About twenty years ago, Northern River Otters were restored to the Rio Grande Wild and Scenic Rivers. Fly fishing on the Rio Hondo near home, above the confluence with the Rio Grande, I saw one and was thrilled. A few years ago, a sculpture by Diné artist Eddie Shorty called to me at a Millicent Rogers Museum auction. She now stands on our living room coffee table, inspiring with her dynamic presence. We are here with you, she says.

The Strategy of Rewilding

Getting back to Leopold's shovel, for our launching locus, we refer you to Paul Wapner's 2020 succinct book *Is Wildness Over?* After evaluating climate change technology initiatives such as de-extinction, geoengineering, carbon dioxide removal, and solar radiation management, he challenges us to pursue "brave new wildness." With appeal to ethics and social justice, this means giving up the dreams of mastery and remaking of the world in our own image. Paul describes "Rewilding" as a strategy, but not a solution guarantee. Key elements are 1) climate mitigation, 2) ecosystem preservation, 3) enhancing nonhuman life, and 4) moral sensitivity to consequences of human actions.

Other thinkers have also proposed guides. Paul Kingsnorth in his 2017 *Confessions of a Recovering Environmentalist* offered these personal practices for our ecological crisis: 1) preserve nonhuman life, 2) root oneself in the work of land and place, 3) insist that Nature has intrinsic value, 4) build refuges where nonhuman life can flourish, and 5) withdraw periodically so you can allow yourself to sit back quietly and feel, intuit, work out what is right for you, and what Nature might need from you.

John Tallmadge's chapter "Towards an Urban Practice of the Wild" appears in Gavin Van Horn and John Hausdoerffer's 2017 *Wildness: Relations of People and Place.* Called "disciplines," he articulates: 1) mindfulness, 2) attentiveness, 3) husbandry, 4) pilgrimage, and 5) witness.

Legions of writers have interpreted Wild far better than we can. The classic ecology philosophers Thoreau, Muir, and Leopold gave their definitions. The etymology is Middle English *wild*, Old English *wilde*, and Proto-Indo-European *wel*, referring to hair, wool, grass, and forest. There are many cognate variations in related languages. Checking the Merriam-Webster Dictionary online, we find the first definition as "In a state of nature, not under human control or care." The second is "Growing or produced in nature." The third is "not civilized, savage, uncontrolled, unruly." There are more, but we'll stop to make a point and observe significantly different value judgments among the definitions. Applied to humans and our attitudes, the root connotation is autonomy and unique self-expression. A more modern psychological term may be uninhibited, as in letting go of contrived restrictions. Poets like Gary Snyder addressed the dualism and separation from wildness imposed by human cultures. Wild became associated with the forbidden, dangerous, inferior, less than human. This meaning is clearly a moral change made by humans. *Homo sapiens* must be vulnerable to a call of the wild seduction.

In the Southwest, the Spanish word *cimarron* was applied to wild, rough, uncouth people. *Wild* is often thought in error to be synonymous with *native*. We have a local river named Cimarron. New Mexico trout there illustrate the differences. Native means originating here, such as Rio Grande cutthroat trout. Wild describes living and reproducing freely, although exotic in origin, such as German brown trout. Native is usually wild, but wild is not necessarily native.

However, man has complicated the natural history of wild trout in several ways. When nineteenth century railroads reached New Mexico, brook trout from New England, brown trout from Europe, and rainbow trout from the Pacific Northwest were brought here as sporting and commercial crops. These newcomers competed for habitat resources with the natives. Stocked rainbows became wild and bred with the native cutthroats, diluting their species' gene pool. Modern technology has produced a sterile rainbow trout that is now raised in hatcheries for angling sport without compromising the genome and vitality of wild native fish. Cutthroat traditional habitat is being restored by programs to remove invasive fish and stock hatchery-raised native fingerlings to live wild. Unfortunately, climate change has warmed some traditional habitat waters, reducing wild reproduction by the colder adapted species. For those of us who fish, and our grandchildren, there still can be some wildness in the sporting experience. Currently in New Mexico, this is not limited to the wilderness

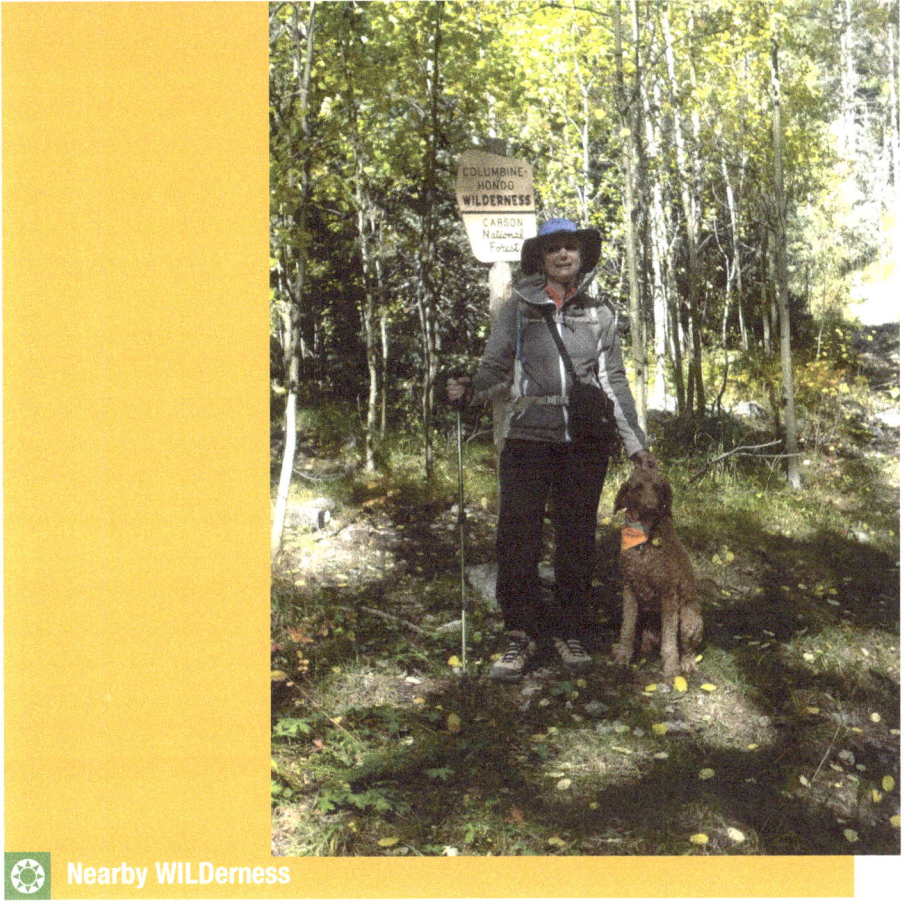

Nearby WILDerness

adventures of the affluent and physically rugged, but also provided in public ponds that allow more egalitarian access. Yes, recreational fishing can have social justice aspects.

What is Wildness?

Recent popular culture portrays wild as a rebellious lifestyle. The *Easy Rider* movie anthem "Born to be Wild" played during a nearby Monument Valley scene celebrated motorcycles on the open road, not Nature. Perceiving value in the original autonomy meaning, Taos writer Mirabai Starr includes *wild* as a quality of modern feminist identity in her 2019 *Wild Mercy*. Indigenous scholar Enrique Salmon describes the absence of distinction between natural wild and humans in other cultures and languages. He names people with a worldview separated from Nature as "Homo modernus industrialii," quoted in Van Horn and Hausdoerffer, op. cit. Others have pursued creative ecoadventures to experience "more than human life" such as David Abram communicating with animals in Bali, described in his 1997 *The Spell of the Sensuous*. In his 2020 *Becoming Wild,* Carl Safina informs us of animal cultures' distinctive qualities.

Our stories travel an odyssey as we attempt to apply qualities of wildness to ecological restoration and regeneration in our quotidian life. Consider this a journal of our practices to enhance the wild qualities in our homeplace homespace. We will refer in the narrative to several excellent texts that inform what you can do. We are primarily describing what we did do and the outcomes. We hope they have rewilding qualities because we are enhancing ecosystem regeneration, rooting in the work of land and place, and attempting mindful husbandry, to use some of our teachers' phrases. We have emphasized New Mexico voices, including community citizens who have been here for centuries, literary geniuses, thoughtful friends and neighbors, and regional scholars.

Journals of rewilding practices applicable to homelife in small spaces seem few. We are among the many people who do not manage commercial farms, conduct professional demonstration programs, produce popular media, teach from institutions, officiate in organized religion, or create ecospiritual retreats. You may also perceive in our narrative the effects on us by these personal practices. Taos Diné teacher Pat McCabe describes this as reciprocal medicine. Potawatomi botany scholar Robin Wall Kimmerer calls this restorative reciprocity. Northern New Mexico has profound traditions of human relationship to the land. More on this in Chapter 1.

Some writers equate ecological progress with preservation of wilderness. Likely not the first to do this parsing, we seek modest **wilder**ness. In our 2020 book, *Taos Horno Adventures: A Multicultural Culinary Memoir Informed by History and Horticulture,* we found popular interest in describing the explorations and innovations of our culinary homelife. We focus now on wild influences and activities that have shaped our ecologic practices. Some are happy reminiscence stories, some describe our methods, and some are attempts to evaluate our outcomes. We offer narratives of homelife and include the efforts of some other conscious practitioners like ourselves. Overall, we are attracted to the idea of Rewilding as personal and productive, even procreative for environmental change.

Wrestling with Abraham

Before we get to the stories of our shovel work, some inner exploration of our conditioned human bias seems needed, as in Wapner's call for awareness of moral consequences. Someone said that an expanded consciousness often leads to a sharpened conscience. Can we rewild and honor the familiar medical dictum *primum non nocere*, "first do no harm"?

Such concerns prompted this reflective essay I call "Wrestling with Abraham." For several years, I have assisted the US Forest Service as volunteer at Aldo Leopold's first home nearby Taos in Tres Piedras. Leopold had built a craftsman style cabin in 1912 for his new wife Estella when he was promoted to Supervisor of the Carson National Forest. From an old New Mexico Hispanic land grant family, she named it *Mi Casita,* my little house. As a free-range volunteer, I have come to know the nooks and crannies as restored to original

Mi Casita

condition in 2007. My dog and I monitor the corral and utility buildings in this National Historic Site, explore a millennium of archaeology in the adjacent rocks, trap numerous invading mice, and often recruit friends for maintenance of the outside woodwork.

I have had the fortunate opportunity to read much that Leopold wrote and literature about him by others in my initiative to develop a library at the cabin. My experience also includes helping support the diverse residents who stay for a creative month through the Albuquerque-based Leopold Writing Program. I learn much from their modern adaptations of his thought. As the cabin is restricted from public access, I appreciate the Forest Service volunteer opportunity and relationship with this legacy.

Leopold states in the Foreword to his 1949 classic *A Sand County Almanac:*

> Conservation is getting nowhere because it is incompatible with our Abrahamic concept of land. We abuse land because we regard it as a commodity belonging to us. When we see land as a community to which we belong, we may begin to use it with love and respect. There is no other way for land to survive the impact of mechanized man, nor for us to reap from it the esthetic harvest it is capable, under science, of contributing to culture.

This assertion has been powerful in my personal response to environmental issues. I call this essay "Wrestling with Abraham" because it provokes concern about the influence of our Judeo-Christian-Muslim heritage. Much as Jacob wrestled with the angel (Genesis 32:25–28), some say out of guilt for his aggrandizing deception of his brother Esau, I think Aldo similarly wrestled with guilt about environmental harm humans have caused from revering Abraham as Patriarch. Not easily ignored in modern life, Abraham's story is often repeated in worship services and Bible studies. In addition to Jewish theology, Bruce Feiler describes Abraham as also the spiritual forefather of the New Testament and the grand holy architect of the Koran in his 2002 *Abraham: A Journey to the Heart of Three Faiths.*

I am moved to also wrestle with this powerful assertion by Leopold, explore his intention, and consider the implications for our environmental progress. How much is his view of Abrahamic values sociologic insight, academic analysis, political assertion, cultural attitude, or personal theology? We can begin with the biblical material he is addressing. The Protestant King James translation of Genesis 1:26 states,

> So God created man in his image, male and female he created them. And God blessed them, and God said unto them, Be fruitful and multiply, and replenish the earth and subdue it: and have

dominion over the fish of the sea and over the fowl of the air, and
over every living thing that moveth upon the earth.

A more recent Jewish translation, Conservative denomination
The Holy Scriptures (Philadelphia, 1917) also says *"domin-
ion."* I note the word's origin is Latin for lord or master, then
carried into Middle English. The 1981 Reform denomination
Union of American Hebrew Congregations' text *The Torah:
A Modern Commentary* has a minimal translation change to
"They shall rule the fish ..." etc.

I perceive a source for Abraham's attitude of land entitlement
in the *King James Bible* Genesis verse 12:1, "Now the Lord
said to Abram, Get thee out of thy country and from thy father's house to a land that I will show thee." And in 12:7, after
arrival in Canaan, "And the Lord appeared unto Abram and
said, Unto thy seed will I give this land." More than ownership, the Hebrew God is said to give a powerful mandate and
protection decree in the promised land:

I will make of you a great nation, And I will bless you; I will
make your name great, and you shall be a blessing. I will bless
those who bless you and curse him that curses you; And all the
families of the earth shall bless themselves by you.

From this, we can see the powerful appeal of subsequent generations believing in human entitlement regarding Nature. I
also find that Abraham asserts a right to land ownership in the
burial of his wife Sarah. Living in Hebron among the Hittites,
Abraham is offered the gift of a place, the Cave of Mach-
pelah, by King Ephron. However, Abraham insists on ownership justified by purchase. This action has set precedents for
both legal and religious possession of land.

How can we relate this biblical history to Aldo Leopold? He
appears to blame the Abrahamic religions' influence on human behavior for exploitation of our biosphere. Can we eval-

uate Leopold's assertion better from biography? Curt Meine in his 1988 *Aldo Leopold: His Life and Work* reports that both grandfathers emigrated from Germany and achieved success in Missouri and Iowa. While holidays were celebrated,

> none of the family attended church on a regular basis. Charles Starker [maternal grandfather and family patriarch] was ostensibly a Lutheran, but not a churchgoer. Carl Leopold [father of Aldo] took a dim view of preachers of any ilk. The children were not influenced in any particular direction in their spiritual development, but left to their own devices, and their own conclusions.

Where then may we look to understand Leopold's Abrahamic religious knowledge? We have a few references to Leopold's religious education from adolescence to later life when he formulated *A Sand County Almanac*. His classes at the Lawrenceville School included Bible study. A letter home in 1905 shows an evolution of consciousness from religion to naturalist in his enjoyment of the emerging Spring: "I wonder if the Holy Land is blessed with such a Resurrection of Nature as occurs with us here at this season."

During the first year at Yale, he attended an elective Bible study class. In 1911, when he was assigned to the Carson National Forest and courted Estella in Santa Fe, she coaxed him into attending church for the first time. Maria Alvira Estella Luna Bergere was a practicing Spanish-Italian Catholic. This is reported of no concern to Aldo. At their Saint Francis Cathedral wedding, Aldo had to vow not to interfere in the spiritual upbringing of their children. Meine reports he was annoyed but cooperative. After his 1914 recovery from life-threatening kidney failure and a required move to an office position in Albuquerque, Leopold began to read, in company with Estella, more literature and philosophy, and especially the Bible.

How has Leopold's Abrahamic assertion been subsequently viewed? Taos interspiritual writer Mirabai Starr in her 2012 *God of Love: A Guide to the Heart of Judaism, Christianity, and Islam* states that the passages about man's dominion have been exploited by all three monotheistic religions as an excuse for devastating the environment. She asserts that dominion implies our challenge "to serve the Divine by taking care of the land and all things that dwell with us here." As discussed by Neal Loevinger in Rabbi Ellen Bernstein's 2000 *Ecology and the Jewish Spirit,* the Deep Ecology movement goes further to assert that

> all of Western religion stands in the way of a more balanced relationship with Nature. The core idea of Deep Ecology is *biocentrism* which finds value in the biological web of life itself, not in humans as a special or unique species.

Some scholars and clergy defend the Abrahamic religions by citing the Bible (Psalms and Book of Job) that express benevolence and more humble relationship values. Genesis 2:15 suggests a command for *stewardship.* In the Protestant King James Bible, man is placed in Eden "to dress it and keep it." The Reform Jewish translation reads "to till it and tend it." Scholars of the biblical documentary thesis attribute these differences in Genesis 1 to later redacting writers.

Speaking out of study in my own Hebraic culture, I find that greatly esteemed Rabbis Moses Maimonides and Abraham Joshua Heschel define human responsibility for care of the Earth as fundamentally a devotion to God. Recent commentators Dan Fink and Marc Swetlitz discuss these theological views in Ellen Bernstein's *Ecology and the Jewish Spirit.* David Gedzelman describes the writings of A. D. Gordon who expressed his twentieth century Zionism as practices linking ourselves to nature through work on the land "as a way of being." I perceive that Leopold was articulating a different dynamic, informed by his evolving ecologic systems thinking, that progress requires direct commitment to the land without a divine factor. In addition to *why* we practice a land ethic, be devoted to *how*.

But while stewardship includes responsibility, it still is defined as management of property, an agency of control. I suggest that attitude may be a slippery slope leading to colonization. This is distinct from the humility of shared community. I think stewardship still implies a dualistic separation between superior caretaker humans and inferior nature. I recognize the distinction between Written Law and Natural Law as the basis for spiritual consciousness and land ethic practice. In my unabridged 1966 Random House Dictionary, the first definition of the word *naturalize* is based on Written Law, "to confer citizenship on an alien." Only in the fourth definition do we learn the meaning "to bring into conformity with Nature."

I recognize another clue to Leopold's thinking in the statement: "There are two things that interest me: the relation of people to each other, and the relation of people to the land." Therefore, I view his Abrahamic reference as not religious or historic criticism, but a psychosocial observation. Maybe I can label it ecosociology. In pursuit of rewilding, I see the dominion theology as control of the wild in all life. It also suggests the entitlement in human attitudes. I perceive this currently in the special qualities people ascribe to experiences in Nature, especially recreation and tourism. Yet recent views of social justice recognize the exclusiveness and economic discrimination in wilderness access promotion. We need to beware the gentrification of "being in Nature." For me then, challenging the dominion claim also becomes a wrestling challenge to achieve progress in our struggle for land ethic relationship and practices. The wild is not isolated to a separate Nature, but inherent to humans as blended with larger Nature. I learned in a Unity service that *privileged* people should distinguish *gratitude* from *entitlement*. Like Jacob with the angel, this consciousness can serve to motivate humans for preserving the integrity, stability, and beauty of the biotic community, as Aldo advocated.

Moving Forward

In closing this Introduction, here is some orientation to our book: this journal surveys one couple's ecological experiences over decades, with a view to pursuit of **wilder**ness, both intentional and intuitive. Our Rewilding actions seek restoration and preservation environmental outcomes. Many of these anecdotes may seem mundane, even trivial, but our purpose is to report on the real, not entertain or instruct about the elaborate or ideal.

Richard is the primary narrator but Annette guided and harmonized the voice. She also designed the photographs, all taken by us. References are not rigorously attributed by academic standards as many are from impressions and experience memories. In addition to our own stories, we sought contribution from others devoted to the human-nature relationship and environmental practices. Veteran journalist Nancy Jeffrey helped our style speak to readers. In addition, as the manuscript matured, we added new wild observations in our homescape. These experiences confirm for us how Rewilding is a dynamic process, a cultivated intuition practice.

We hope some readers will join us in seeking pragmatic ways to accomplish ecological benefits in small spaces. Some homescaping friends observed this book can be a reference. Therefore, we added an index, not encyclopedic, but organized in categories to follow our usefulness intention.

✱ **Our Homescape**

Place is important to our initiatives and consciousness, recognized locally in New Mexico as the qualities of *querencia*. More than possession, this term evokes communal relationship. Therefore, we inform our stories with northern New Mexico culture that illustrates peoples' relationship to the land. However, we also offer our narrative as models for practices anywhere as we wander about among our wilder experiences. So, let's take a walk together on the Rewilding side!

Remembering Our Land's Wildness

There were people in the mountain landscape whom I could not ignore. They had used the land and ultimately altered it. Even more interesting was the question of how the land had altered them, how natural history had shaped the history of cultures. William deBuys, *River of Traps,* 1990.

We believe one way to increase consciousness and practice of Rewilding is through understanding the past human-land relationship, the centuries of community with the land. Beyond thinking of what people did on the land, let's consider what the land did for our human predecessors. This is definitely not depreciative of these people as inferior wild.

Annette and I built our house on high plains at 7,200 feet, before the foothills ascend El Salto Peak to the east towards the Wheeler Peak Wilderness. Before houses, the land was upland grass and sage used for animal grazing the past 350 years. The Rio Grande Gorge runs north to south about

✪ El Salto and Lake Fork Ridge Alpenglow

ten miles to the west and our view there extends for a hundred miles.

To understand the people who lived here before, we draw from several sources. David Stuart, Senior Scholar at the University of New Mexico School for Advanced Research, provides extensive documentation in his 2014 *Anasazi America*. We add a description of traditional plant gathering and cultivation practices from Lisa Rayner's 2013 *Growing Food in the Southwest Mountains*. Last, my friend and neighbor James C. Bull produced a small but powerful history book *Out of Time* about our hometown, Arroyo Seco, in 1998 to benefit restoration of its historic church. He wisely included the wisdom of local sages such as *Norteños* Larry Torres and Pablo Quintana; Barbara Waters, the spouse of esteemed writer Frank; and Bruce Gomez from Taos Pueblo, among others. Passing suddenly in recent weeks, I miss sharing this Rewilding literary expedition with Jim.

Here are selected words from Jim's book describing the setting of our homescape:

> The magical El Salto de las Aguas and Lucero Peak situated east of town have numerous waterfalls, visible in the spring. They capture the winter snowfall so that the Arroyo Seco Creek and the conjoining Rio Lucero Ditch can fill the *acequias*. Cottonwoods and willows that line the creek and the *acequias* become golden in the fall and define the banks. The Winter sun sets behind Pedernal butte at the western village of Abiquiu.

The People Who Came Before Us

Let's explore what historians and archaeologists are thinking now about the first people to live in the Southwestern United States. We learn from artifacts that have been protected by state and federal government laws. The definition is not strict and favors leaving artifacts in place for study, particularly on Federal lands, but not private.

A personal learning story about this: on a field trip to the Stewart Meadows Ranch Preserve led by a US Forest Service guide, I was being a good scout picking up things like water bottles and soda cans left by tourists and hunters. When I picked up a rusty can, the guide Bonnie told me that if I could read a label, it was trash. But if rusted and unidentifiable, leave it alone as an artifact.

The first Federal Law Antiquities Act in 1906 addressed formation of national monuments to protect natural, cultural, and scientific features. This was confirmed in the 1976 Federal Land Policy Management Act. Native American artifacts on federal and tribal lands are protected by the 1979 Archaeological Resources Protection Act and the 1990 Native American Graves Protection and Repatriation Act.

In recounting this chronology, we intentionally omit most classification names, to respect the diverse and often controversial views about the ancestor peoples' identities. We think about how we have been similar rather than separate from others. The Clovis People were believed the first to live in the Southwest, so named because their spear points and stone tools were discovered in 1932 near Clovis, NM. Scientists dated them to about 13,000 years ago.

However, new discoveries in many places around North and South America from the Arctic to Chile have pushed back the time of the first ancient people to 30,000 years ago. It is possible they may have been in the Taos Valley. Based on DNA evidence, some scientists say 80 percent of modern Native Americans descended from them. They were skilled hunters and pursued animals now extinct such as mammoths, mastodons, and camelops. Archaeologists believe the Clovis People then migrated to South America but mysteriously vanished, likely joining with other groups.

As the climate warmed, the Ice Age large animals were replaced by smaller bison, deer, elk, bear, and bighorn sheep. People then moved their camps often to hunt these herds. About 7,000 years ago, the climate began to show seasonal changes and became drier. Grass grew less and the bison herds moved further north. This prompted the people to change their tools. Plant gathering became more important than animal hunting for food. In spring, they moved up into the mid-elevations, gathered leafy greens, and dug roots such as yampa, camas bulbs, and wild onion. They developed different cooking methods, such as hot stones in a skin-lined pit to boil water. Often these smooth stones cracked from the heat, and fire stone artifacts now show us where people lived.

More available plant and animal food in the warmer weather helped population increase in the New Mexico region. They spent more settled time in certain places to find and prepare food. Seeds were ground to flour with hand grinder *manos* on stone bowl *metates*. In wetter mountain areas, acorns and piñon nuts were eaten. By 3,500 years ago, people did more deliberate farming when rain increased. Corn, properly called maize, was introduced from Mexico. Squash and beans were first grown about 2,500 years ago. These new foods made the peoples' diets healthier. In summer, families travelled into the high elevations to collect berries and seeds such as sunflower, amaranth, and ricegrass. Sweet sap was tapped from pine and aspen trees. People often moved in different seasons, leaving artifacts of many thousand small pithouses. Hunting improved about 2,000 years ago with the use of bows and arrows, learned from the northern Great Plains tribes.

Settlements in the Wild

In the next 500 years, while foraging and hunting were still done seasonally, settlements made more permanent farming areas possible. Basketmaker crafts of plant material have been found protected in caves. People would travel out to farm plots and sleep in small pithouses during the growing season. These were dug into the ground, then covered with tree branch walls and roof. Pithouses evolved to continuous use and expanded to include storage places for food.

Social customs also developed, such as establishing nearby burial places. Pottery use began in the New Mexico area about 1,600 to 1,700 years ago. The knowledge of how to make pottery came from people in northern Mexico and eastern Arizona regions. Pots made cooking quicker, easier, and more efficient. New farm animals included turkeys, brought north from Central and South America. The eggs for food and feathers for blankets were most valued. Feathers were woven together with rabbit fur and yucca fibers to make winter clothing.

Pithouses in group settlements became similar and construction qualities improved. As communities lived together, more religious practices and forms of craft developed. Trading was done across larger distances, as shown by types of beads and different pottery designs we can find now. Archaeologists have been able to determine when and where different pottery was made from the study of sherds.

More people moved to uplands to farm near better water sources. Sometimes groups also chose areas on higher ground to protect themselves from others' attacks to steal food. Square rooms were built above ground to store foods such as corn and beans. These were put into large jars for protection from rain and rodents. The style of storage room construction is called *jacal*, meaning mud plastered upright poles with a roof of saplings, also covered with mud. The people would sleep and cook in pithouses located in front of these jacal rooms.

Because the numbers of people increased, but climate changes made farming and hunting practices unreliable, many more settlements were established over larger areas. Trading of food such as corn and beans, tools, and pottery was also active among these farmstead Pueblos. We can identify many different pottery styles by their uses and decoration. The building methods became more permanent, particularly storage rooms of stone grouped together. Ceremonial kiva rooms first appeared then.

However, when the Chaco culture in western New Mexico declined about 900 years ago, many people left their large communities and moved to uplands where there was more water for farming. Instead of great houses as at Chaco, they returned to living in small pithouses. Certain areas were not open to them, because Pueblos had been established earlier, particularly in the Taos and Jemez areas.

Understanding the Homes

Numerous small pithouse sites have been discovered and documented near our home on the El Prado and Arroyo Seco high prairies. The New Mexico State Historical Preservation Office records indicate several dozen sites nearby. These are described as Precontact, meaning before arrival of the Spanish in 1598, and show evidence of pithouses, human burials, roomblock structures, fire-cracked rock, and areas of ceramic and stone tool scatter. The later Postcontact period is called Historic, and evidence includes Hispanic adobe mounds, abandoned irrigation *acequias*, trash dumps, and dung hill middens. Many of the sites have both ancient and historic evidence, as successive people camped and lived in these places.

How might the early pithouses have looked? Archaeologist Michael Burney provided us an article from the Taos County Historical Society (*Ayer y Hoy en Taos*, Issue No. 43, Fall 2017) by Skip Miller, former archaeologist for the Carson National Forest:

Between about 950 and 1050 C.E., the first permanent settlements were established in the Taos Valley. These early, year-round residents built deep pit-house dwellings. Using simple wooden digging sticks, they often excavated pits that ranged from six to more than eight feet below the surface and were from thirteen to twenty or more feet across. The pit houses were roofed with a cribbed or layered arrangement of pinon and juniper poles covered with a thick layer of plant material and several feet of dirt. All this was supported internally by a framework of large posts and beams, similar in configuration to the earth lodges of the Great Plains. Access to these completely subterranean structures was from a stepped-pole ladder through a central hole in the roof.

Historical reports describe that the building of Taos Pueblo began about year AD 1000 (1000 CE) by the Northern Tiwa tribe. Differences in family and tribe groups still existed then in the widespread settlements outside the Pueblo, including many pit-house groups.

Post-Contact Changes

The first Hispanic explorer to reach Taos Valley was Capitan Hernando Alvarado on August 29, 1540. He was part of the expedition led by Francisco Vasquez de Coronado. By 1615, the village of Taos was established with an appointed *alcalde* (mayor or municipal magistrate). Then followed the difficult story of Governor Don Juan Oñate and the Pueblo Revolt led by Po'pay in 1680, the reconquest by Don Diego de Vargas, and the final surrender of Taos Pueblo in 1696. According to Jim Bull's research, in 1697 there were apparently only 1,500 Spanish-speaking persons in the New Mexico colony of New Spain. By 1790, the Hispanic population had increased to 15,000.

Giving the Land Titles

Focusing on our home location, the Arroyo Seco land grant previously ceded to Lucero de Godoy was occupied by Don Antonio Martinez who received a regrant from the New Spain governor on October 26, 1716. The Martinez heirs settled the area below El Salto and Lucero peaks. For protection against raiding parties of nomadic Native Americans, a *torreon* watch tower was built near El Salto in approximately 1745, according to archaeological surveys by Jeffrey Boyer. The first *ace-*

Grazing Now

quia irrigation systems were developed in the later 1700s, and farm crops were documented in the early 1800s.

Coronado's 1540 expedition brought 5,000 hardy churro breed sheep to supply the soldiers with meat. Oñate brought 3,000 more in 1598. Sheep ranching became the major source of both small subsistence income and large wealth. The land grant patrons further south included the Luna family of Estella Leopold. They began moving large herds to California to feed the Gold Rush miners. In 1852, "Mountain Man" Dick Wooten drove 9,000 sheep from Taos to Sacramento, California. Kit Carson drove 6,500 sheep there in 1853. When the Colorado gold rush started in 1858, sheep herds were driven north to feed the many miners.

Men from the small villages of northern New Mexico worked as sheepherders in the open forests where more grass and water were available during the summer months. We understand them better from carved aspen trees with their names, home villages, and religious symbols. These arborglyph artifacts have been recorded by historians and the US Forest Service.

After the sheep were sold, herders would come back to their home villages, including those in the Taos Valley, for the winter. However, by the 1890s, Taos Mesa had been overgrazed by sheep, eliminating the native grasses such as grama, brome, bluestem, and muttongrass. Big sagebrush has become the main plant filling empty spaces. While native to much of the southwest and northern plains, scholars report that many more seeds were brought by the thousands of horses imported from California. They were driven on the Old Spanish Trail between Los Angeles and Santa Fe. We also have much rubber rabbit-brush, locally called *chamisa,* that has spread throughout the overgrazed fields.

Cultures Coexisting

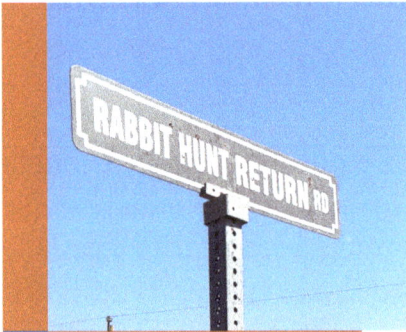

Rabbit Hunt Today

For hundreds of years, the Taos Pueblo Annual Rabbit Hunt was held across the nearby open plains, including our land. Our home is two miles from Pueblo fields. Carmela Quinto, the former curator at Millicent Rogers Museum, reports that the rabbit hunt extended across the open llano plains to the west until 2007. Houses and fences have limited it to smaller Reservation areas now, but I have observed that it still occurs. This is an interesting ritual between humans and small mammals: part social contest, part food gathering, and part protection of the Pueblo farm crops.

When the Mexican Independence Revolution in 1821 opened the northern and eastern New Spain borders, traders and trappers of northern European blood came to the Taos Valley. They liked to camp around Turley's Mill, drink Taos Lightning moonshine, trade, gamble, and compete in skill contests. The Turleys were brothers from Missouri who built a trading post and flour mill on the nearby Rio Hondo in 1830.

During the Mexican American War in 1847, Pueblo and Hispanic fighters attacked the settlement and killed most of the men. This was called the Taos Rebellion and included the murder of New Mexico colony Governor Charles Bent. The mill site is now listed in the National Register of Historic Places. The only other Anglo registered historic site from this time is the Kit Carson house in Taos town. For a more colorful and detailed history with environmental consciousness, see John Nichols' 1994 *If Mountains Die.*

Arroyo Seco Life Now

Jim Bull records that historic homes dating to the nineteenth century are still located on the north side of El Salto Road. The south side of the road is a parcel of Taos Pueblo land referred to as the Tenorio Tract. It was transferred to the Pueblo in 1934 following a Federal court decision involving title to the property they claimed to have purchased from Spanish settlers over 100 years earlier for 5,500 pesos.

The stories of twentieth century Taos and environs are still prominent in our journalism and literature. The traditional northern Hispanic villages have a powerful cultural legacy. Thinking of people's relationship to the land, here is testimony from Frank Waters' 1941 classic novel *People of the Valley:*

> There are many earths, and each has its own irreconcilable spirit of place. Now what is a man but his earth? It rises in walls to shelter him in life. It sinks to receive him at death. By eating its corn, he builds his flesh into walls of this selfsame earth. He has its granitic hardness or its soft resiliency. He is different as each field is different. This do I know of my own earth; I can know no other.

Surviving through the national struggles of World War I, the Depression, and World War II, we recognize local Taos changes of the artist colony, celebrity notoriety, US Government Federal lands management conflicts, ski valley development, tourism, and hippie presence. Creative and passionate voices like Aldo Leopold and D. H. Lawrence described the local wildness. As consumerism and extraction industries have been destructive of the land's vitality, we now turn our Rewilding stories toward restoration and regeneration. However, this should be more than a common call for stewardship. Yes, that is utilitarian, caretaking agency but it may also enable anthropocentric sovereignty attitudes. Humans may not know better than Gaia. In *Rewilding,* we recognize her autonomy.

In his 2019 book *Think Little,* Buddhist farmer poet Wendell Berry said:

> We have lived by the assumption that what was good for us would be good for the world.… We have been wrong.… For I do not doubt that it is only on the condition of humility and reverence before the world that our species will be able to remain in it.

In Community with Trees

It is not until the transect is completed that the tree falls, and the stump yields a collective view of a century. By its fall, the tree attests to the unity of the hodge-podge called history. Aldo Leopold, *A Sand County Almanac,* 1949.

When engaged in the drafting of this chapter, we realized that Tu B'Shvat is soon, the fifteenth of the month of Shvat in the ancient Hebrew lunar calendar. This was established in the biblical kingdom era as the birthday of all cultivated trees so that a tax of produce could be collected when the trees reached their fourth year. However, prior to this economic management of agriculture, in times of more pastoral life, the season was celebrated for the renewal signaled by the first tree budding in the Middle East, usually almonds. This had sacred meaning in the old Hebrew oral tradition, eventually written into Genesis. The importance of trees was profound.

A teaching we recently received from modern Hasidic Rabbi Gershon Winkler relates that "Tree is older than Sun and Moon and Stars and Planets." In the biblical Genesis story, Tree is created in the third day cycle, whereas Sun does not appear until the fourth, making Tree

> representative of the Point of Beginning within which Creator sowed the seeds of endless possibility in the rest of the story: stars, creeping-crawlies, fish, animals, birds, insects—until we get to Human, who, like Tree, is created singular.... And so, the Bible calls Human "the Tree of the Field."

We relate this teaching to suggest sources of the spiritual power and ecocentric relationship we can feel with trees. A personal anecdote: my astute son-in-law and daughter are living in an old Philadelphia suburb, near his childhood home. Their house is surrounded by several dozen tall trees. These various oaks are likely second growth from original farm clearing two hundred years ago. During a visit, he commented, "You seem to think about trees a lot." I realized he was accustomed to living in a magnificent forest, different from our high desert plains usually tree bare.

Arboreal Rewilding at Home

Back to our home experience, the half-acre had been devoid of trees for indeterminate decades. The area was likely open grazing fields for sheep and cattle on the outskirts of Arroyo Seco village. After the native grasses were overgrazed, big sagebrush, *Artemisia tridentata,* and rabbitbrush, *Ericameria nauseosa,* became dominant. In addition, European alfalfa was introduced as a feed crop. It spread as an invasive beyond

El Salto de las Aguas

the cultivated fields. Our land had been irrigated by *acequias* off the El Salto systems, but traditional rights to share this water were sold before our neighborhood houses were built, requiring us to allow flow through to downstream *parciente* irrigators.

Our house builder planted five trees on the lot's front swale: a native piñon, *Pinus edulis*, a native ponderosa, *Pinus ponderosa*, two imported Scotch pines, *Pinus sylvestris*, and an aspen, *Populous tremuloides*. The spring we closed on the house, we planted two ponderosas and an aspen immediately behind the house facing west. We consider these eight trees our original arboreal family.

How are they faring now, twenty-nine years later? Trees have their own personalities if we inquire. Paul Bryan Jones, certified arborist who chaired the Town of Taos Tree Board, said in answer to frequent questions about where to plant, "The tree will tell you." In our semiarid neighborhood at 7,200 feet, the transplanted aspens have been at risk, particularly on those lots with second home absentee owners. Through cycles of drought years, many have died. They flourish in the moist meadows and mountain crevasses high above us. However, our tree's placement close to the crowned road runoff and my periodic hose watering saved our original aspen at the front of the house. As aspens do, it has propagated two additional trunks. Aspens are not solitary trees but develop extensive root systems that can produce multiple new trunk shoots. That is why now, in our neighborhood many clumps of smaller trees have grown in wetter years from the roots of the originals that were cut down after their crowns' death. A contender for the largest biomass organism on Earth is a stand of aspens in Utah. And the aspen tree we planted behind the house on the west side has thrived from roof runoff water, now the thickest trunk and tallest crown in the neighborhood.

Here's a meaningful aspen tree experience. In 1996, a forest fire threatened the Lama Foundation Spiritual Center about thirty miles north of Taos. Originally organized as an inter-spiritual commune, the residents' water came from a historic spring that was enclosed in a protective stone structure. About seventeen years after the fire, I attended a Contemplative Environmental Practice Retreat led by Paul Wapner. One of our sylvan experience hikes went to the springhouse. Many acres of tall ponderosa, Douglas fir, and aspen had been burned, and pioneer Gambel oak were growing back, then just a few feet tall. However, hundreds of adolescent aspens from the surviving root matrix were growing in the cleft above the spring, a wild forest restoration. In that same retreat, a botanist explained why aspens quake. They evolved a petiole leaf attachment that allows both sides to be exposed to the sun in a breeze. This increases the amount of photosynthesis food production for more rapid growth.

What about our original family ponderosas planted near the house's west side? Aside from a few old cottonwoods on the nearest *acequia*, they are now the tallest, thickest trees in sight. We figure this is a blessing of community: water from the roof runoff, plus warmth and wind protection from the adobe walls. Maybe our human company and admiration add vitality. We appreciate the useful winter fireplace kindling provided by their autumn cone shedding. And we have all learned much from Peter Wohlleben's 2015 *The Hidden Life of Trees: What They Feel, How They Communicate.* Maybe these two ponderosas are glad to have a friend, maybe considered a mate, thirty feet away, well within root range. The solo tree, planted a year prior on the front swale, is only half their size.

Wind and Water for Fruit

Trees planted on impulse have also been teachers, sometimes with their sacrifice. As the house was a vacation center in our young family years, we often purchased additions but did not consistently tend them. Having grown up with apple trees, we contributed a mature tree to the bare back yard. We enjoyed a couple of spring blossom and late summer fruit years, then our mountain spring hard frosts did their damage, and she did not survive.

Our neighbors, also second homers then, planted several fruit trees behind their house. Only one has made it, still bearing lovely small peaches in some years. It benefits from a roof runoff *canal*. Interestingly, wild plum trees that grow along our roads have sent volunteer sprouts around this lone peach, likely from magpie delivered seeds. What wild community vitality!

We have since learned more about the wind protection and water needs of fruit trees. Peaches, first brought by the Franciscans who accompanied early settlers, have been cultivated in northern New Mexico for over four hundred years. We had an experience of this during our 1970s Albuquerque years. The prior owner of our Baja Corrales *ranchito* planted a peach tree, *Prunus persica.* Originally from the mountains of China and Tibet, they have thrived around the world for over six thousand years. We became acquainted and paid attention to her, particularly the effects of spring frosts on the blossoms. One year, they were luxurious. When a frost threatened, we had the idea of stringing Christmas lights, the old incandescent kind. She rewarded us with abundant large fruit. You may say, this is just your horticulture practice, not wildness. And with a tree originally brought from China! However, we feel more in relationship with a true experience of our shared environment.

Speaking of historic stone fruits, other immigrant trees adapted to the greater Taos Valley and now grow wild. One spring I noticed a tree behind the Leopold Mi Casita cabin with a few unusual blossoms for that setting. On closer exam, it was an apricot, *Prunus armeniaca,* similar to many scattered around the county. Some grow wild along roadsides in Arroyo Seco. The type with small fruits was brought initially by the seventeenth-century Franciscans. After the coming of the railroad, species with larger fruit were brought from California.

With my curiosity aroused, I scouted the area behind the cabin overgrown with Gambel oak and found another tree. Both seemed deliberately placed, flanking the original root cellar. I recruited US Forest Service technician Robin to help my research. Her coring aged the original tree at 85 years, after Leopold's time 108 years ago. However, many Forest Service rangers, staff, and CCC workers have lived in the cabin subsequently. In restoration spirit, I pruned deadwood from these long-neglected trees and cleared sun-blocking scrub oaks. Next season, one rewarded me with a few fruits. As I enjoyed telling this story to cabin visitors in the Leopold Writing Program Residency last October, Emily Wortman-Wunder from Denver discovered a small apricot volunteer forty feet away, likely seeded by a bird or rodent's meal. I am eager to identify this wild gift when it leafs out this spring.

As Pasteur said, "chance favors the prepared mind." I have been historic garden cultivator at the Millicent Rogers Museum in Taos for several years. Primed by the Leopold cabin discovery, I examined trees on the neglected three acres south of the museum more closely. There were remnants of the prior Anderson family home, partcularly a garden wall and *horno.* And *voilá,* hidden behind several volunteer juniper trees, an old apricot had persisted.

After cutting the junipers and pruning dead wood, I recruited Ben Wright, certified arborist from the Taos Land Trust Rio Fernando Restoration, to do a coring. This tree's age was 75, contemporary with the time of the Andersons' residence. Pruned once again in the late winter, this time for productivity, the tree produced an abundant crop of small apricots the next summer. Somewhere between the categories of domestic and wild, I have come to respect the feral nature of many organisms.

Hmm, feral. My 1966 *Random House Unabridged Dictionary* inherited from my father defines *feral* as: 1) existing in a natural state, not domestic or cultivated, and 2) having reverted to a wild state. Wow, going feral seems like Rewilding to me. I think this feral spirit is now on my shoulder watching what I say and do. Maybe it has been there for a while. We'll come back to visit the feral spirit later in this odyssey.

Small Homescape Choices

Naturalized Austrian Pines

Ten years ago, our dream to settle in the Taos house full time for retirement was accomplished, so our arboreal fantasies were energized. What to plant? What qualities do we seek? Aesthetics? Shade? Habitat? Size? Hardiness? Growth rate? Native or adapted Exotic? Where to plant? Water needs? Cost? Availability? Our house south side is fifty feet from a neighbor, so we desired a tree screen. There are good sources of quality trees nearby: Petree's Nursery off Blueberry Hill Road, particularly for larger trees and extensive variety (plus they have a crew for planting); Serna Landscaping in El Prado, which provides transplants from family land in the Mora Valley; and Gordon Tooley in Truchas, who specializes in natives and organic grafted fruit trees, particularly apples. We avoid commercial nurseries and box stores where the sources and cultivation toxicity are unknown. Considering hardiness, appearance, availability, size, and cost, we chose hybrid Austrian pines, *Pinus nigra,* for the south screen.

A story about tree size choice: when Blossom's Nursery in Ranchos de Taos went out of business about twelve years ago, we scored several 18-inch tall Austrians for a few dollars. Along with some common juniper, *Juniperus communis* shrubs, we planted them in an arc on the west side of the garden beds as a potential windbreak. A neighbor chided, "What will you do when they grow to block your view?" Being a soon-to-retire geezer, I answered, "I should live so long." Moral: buy as much tree as you can afford. These small Austrians are now four feet tall and the originally ten-foot southside Austrians are twenty feet, ten years later. None have been lost.

You may ask, isn't a native tree more desirable? And for this essay, does a hybrid choice qualify as Rewilding? We believe it depends on the qualities of the tree. Austrians are similar to native ponderosas and do not impose noxious environmental effects. Not all imports are so benign. Russian olive, *Elaeagnus angustifolia,* is now notorious. Popularly planted a few decades ago in New Mexico as a rapid growing decorative, it spreads intrusively and contains thorns. The commercial sale is controversial.

✿ Southside Pines and Spruce

Another hybrid versus native choice opportunity for us appeared in the spaces between the south side Austrians. Desiring an attractive out-the-window view, I purchased several Vanderwolf's Pyramids, which are classified the same as the native limber pine, *Pinus flexilis*. They are full shaped, with long soft bluish needles. Why the different common name? Yes, you can copyright a plant variation. No downside, and still close to purist native Rewilding.

As the land slopes a few feet from our house pad to the west, half our lot is open on the south and north sides. Along the southern border further out from the house, we also planted tall Austrians, and in between them, four-foot Engelmann spruce, *Picea engelmanii,* obtained from Gordon Tooley. Slower growing, they are now seven feet, but maturing well. This year, dozens of small cones appeared for the first time, announcing their readiness to reproduce. Engelmann spruce are part of so-called mixed conifer habitat we can see above the lower junipers on El Salto Peak to the east and into the Wheeler and Columbine Hondo Wilderness areas to the north. Our homescape residents attune us to recognize the subtleties of their life cycles. As we have been sensitized to these observations, in late spring many conifer species develop growth points on branch ends. These may be small on little white spruce or quite large on the ponderosas and Austrians. Tree provider Mike called them "candles." Now, isn't that illuminating.

Personal Ritual with Trees

Rewilding can be expressed in the significant rituals of personal life. Our oldest son Brady, Albuquerque-born in 1975, had lifelong severe developmental disabilities. These got the better of him nine years ago and let his soul free. Soon after we began full time retirement in the Taos house, we es-

Brady's Bosque

tablished a *descanso* called "Brady's Bosque." According to Ruben Cobos's 1983 *Dictionary of New Mexico and Southern Colorado Spanish,* a *descanso* is a shrine or rest, usually marked by a heap of stones and a wooden cross. These are seen frequently along highways here. However, reflecting our Jewish heritage, we planted ten native Colorado blue spruce, *Picea pungens,* close together in our southwestern corner instead of a cross.

Ten is the traditional number of mourners that sanctify a memorial service, called a *minyan.* In the center of the group within a spruce log tepee frame, we placed a sculpture of *Kokopelli,* the ancient Hohokam hunchback flute player. Originally eighteen inches high, the trees are now seven to eight feet tall. Maybe they, too, appreciate the community closeness. Naturalists have described the phenomenon of a *tree root matrix.* And by the way, *bosque* is Spanish for a

Kokopelli Rainbow

tree grove. In the 1970s, we rode our horses from our Baja Corrales home through the cottonwood bosque along the Rio Grande in the North Valley area called Alameda. New shopping center sprawl now blocks the way.

Like this *Kokopelli* in Brady's Bosque, we think spiritual figures from diverse cultures can be expressions of Rewilding, not to culturally appropriate, but to honor meaningful symbolism. *Kokopelli* has become a cliché in the southwest, even exploited on *t-shirts* and trinkets. However, I was introduced to him by my first Native American teacher, Alfonso Ortiz, from Ohkay Owingeh (formerly called San Juan Pueblo). When Anthropology Dept. faculty at Princeton, Al included me in an initiative for a dozen Anglo students with useful skills to work at the new Rough Rock Demonstration School on the Navajo Nation in 1968. Knowing I was headed to medical school, Al gave me an article from the *Journal of the American Medical Association* describing research on why *Kokopelli's* ancient petroglyph images have a hunchback and a flute. Tuberculosis of the spine, called Pott's Disease, was common among Southwestern tribes, and collapsed vertebrae caused hunchback.

One anthropology view ascribed the flute to the cultural role of hunchbacks becoming minstrels and entertainers, like medieval European dwarf court jesters. However, some petroglyphs show a phallus instead of a flute. It so happens that Pott's disease can cause a male condition known as priapism, an abnormal persistent erection. This may have endowed such men with a reputation for magical fertility powers. One popular novel portrayed *Kokopelli* as a wanderer who spread his seed, and we don't mean for apple trees. A more sanitized commercial version has him with a backpack and flute as a minstrel, not handicapped.

Kokopelli helped us have a tree regeneration experience. The three-foot sculpture was bought about twenty-eight years ago at Phil Bareiss's Gallery nearby, made by Wilson Crawford. This little guy lived on the house patio before moving to Brady's Bosque. The same year we built the Taos house, Hurricane Andrew blew through our Pinecrest, Florida, neighborhood and destroyed dozens of our tall Dade County pines. For our rebuilding and replanting project there in the storm's aftermath, we commissioned Wilson to make a five-foot *Kokopelli* to be stationed on a stump and serenade the new trees. He now stands back here amidst the garden beds and native flowers at the Taos house. Maybe his ancient music we imagine helps inform us of Rewilding values. His seed is now spiritual.

Creating Tree Community

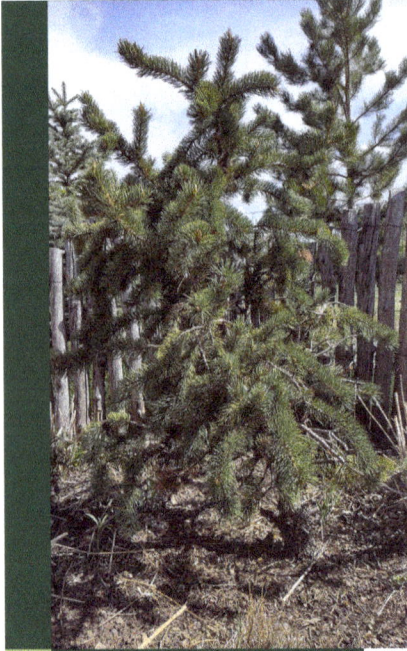
Bristlecone Pine

The tree spirits' influence increased when I became involved in the Taos Chapter of the New Mexico Native Plant Society and discovered Jack Carter's 2012 revised edition text *Trees and Shrubs of New Mexico*. Musing about expanding the trees at home, I learned from Professor Carter that Taos County has thirteen native conifers. Eureka! We had a project to develop a native arboretum. A Leopold restoration influence was also at work here.

When appointed Professor of Game Management at the University of Wisconsin, Leopold was instrumental in establishing the University Arboretum and Wildlife Refuge on a mixed five hundred acres near Madison. According to biographer Curt Meine in his 1988 *Aldo Leopold: His Life and Work*, Leopold envisioned not just a collection of trees, but a re-creation of the land as it once existed, restored with entire plant communities, a "wild institution." Meine reports that in the founding ceremony, Chief Albert Yellow Thunder, a native Ho-Chunk, said: "My people are like the trees, a dying race, leaving behind them as their only monument the natural forests and streams of America." Meine comments: "The Natives, like the wolf, might not return to the land, but the arboretum could at least remind future generations that they were once there."

First, we surveyed what native conifers were already on our half acre. Of the five pines considered natives, we had piñon, ponderosa, and limber. A trip to Petree's Nursery found two tall southwestern white pines, *Pinus strobiformis,* which now live along our western border, inside the *latilla* fence serving as a windbreak. The last needed was a bristlecone, *Pinus aristata*. This is a distinctive tree, living for millennia, and often photographed in wizened shapes. We had visited a stand of bristlecones in the northern New Mexico Valle Vidal Preserve with Bonnie Woods, a Forest Service friend. Yes, that's her real name, given by her carpenter father.

Another memorable experience of bristlecones is a lovely waltz the local trio Rifters play—a dancing favorite. A version is on Jenny Bird's 2010 CD, *Songs of Trees*. Written by Hugh Prestwood, here are the moving lyrics to "Bristlecone Pine."

> Way up in the mountains on the high timber line
> There's a twisted old tree called the Bristlecone Pine
> The wind there is bitter, it cuts like a knife
> And it keeps that tree holding on for dear life.
>
> But hold on it does, standing its ground
> Standing as empires rise and fall down
> When Jesus was gathering lambs to his fold
> The tree was already a thousand years old.
>
> Now the way I have lived, there ain't no way to tell
> When I die if I'm going to heaven or hell.
> So when I'm laid to rest it would suit me just fine
> To sleep at the feet of the Bristlecone Pine
> To sleep at the feet of the Bristlecone Pine.
>
> For as I would slowly return to the earth
> What little this body of mine might be worth
> Would soon start to nourish the roots of that tree
> And it would partake of the essence of me.

And who knows but that as the centuries turn
A small spark of me might continue to burn
As long as the sun did continue to shine
Down on the limbs of the Bristlecone Pine.

Now the way I have lived there ain't no way to tell
When I die if I'm going to heaven or hell
So I'd just as soon serve out eternity's time
Asleep at the feet of the Bristlecone Pine.
Asleep at the feet of the Bristlecone Pine.

One spring day I was scouting the new arrivals at Petree's Nursery and, half joking, asked Mike the proprietor if he had any Bristlecones. He rubbed his chin in thought and said, "Yup, I have one left over from last year in a pot, and I could give you a deal." It turned out this pot was four feet square, holding a tree four feet tall. Mike said it was transplanted from Oregon.

His planting crew established it inside our south fence next to Brady's Bosque. It must be happy there because seven years later it has grown a foot, a lot for a bristlecone. We are happy to have liberated this wild tree from captivity in a nursery pot.

Our next category of native conifers proved easy, as we already established Colorado blue and Engelmann spruce. Moving on to a survey of our Junipers, four low shrub common junipers, *Juniperus communis,* were included in the west garden crescent. As we learned conifer botany in this process, we found the ubiquitous Rocky Mountain *Juniperus scopularum* and one-seeded *Juniperus monosperma* growing wild along the old wire fence on our west boundary where Dadou Meyer used to pasture his horses. One of the original Taos Ski Valley instructors with his brother Jean, he hosted the Salsa del Salto Bed and Breakfast nearby.

The final three items needed for the arboretum were the firs. Here the El Prado Serna Landscape guys proved useful. They had a white fir, *Abies concolor,* and two small corkbark fir, *Abies arizonica,* that transplanted well along the gravel drive-way circle in our house front. Then we learned, checking the various sources, that the Douglas fir, *Pseudostuga menziesii,* that fills western forests is not available commercially taller than a couple of feet. The Serna guys harvested a ten-footer from their Mora Valley family land. Five years later, it has great vitality planted at the crown of our lot's east front swale.

Having too much fun to stop there, we continued to add more native conifers. My karma includes that Earth Day is also my birthday, so each year I buy our small land space presents of trees. Attractive additions have been several limber pines with their long, soft blueish needles. Others were hardy piñon. We hope that several will pollinate each other to produce nuts. The small male cones provide pollen and the larger are fruit-bearing female cones. But a tree does not fertilize itself, only neighbors. Yes, piñons like group sex.

Admittedly proud of this native conifer collection, I offered a field trip to the Taos Native Plant Society. Retired Forest Service botanist Renee Galeano developed Project Pinecone based in Livermore, Colorado. She has assembled a large collection of international pinecone specimens and actively teaches about her passion. Renee led the group on a tour of our home arboretum, and my reward was a bumper sticker of her motto "Fractals from the Forest."

But whoa! Our north side border was still treeless five years ago. Now it accommodates in west-to-east order, a Rocky Mountain juniper, a ponderosa, an Austrian pine, a Rocky Mountain white pine, and two unusually tall piñons. The trees seem to enjoy their diverse neighbors.

Trees can add to the meaning of life events. Last year, our neighbor Jim Bull offered a ponderosa seedling that sprouted under a parent tree he transplanted from his Colorado home twenty-five years ago. We replanted it on the front swale inside a rock border. After the winter snow cover melted, we could recognize a few inches of shoot. As recorded in Chapter 1, Jim suddenly passed in spring of 2021. This ponderosa sprout is now a wild *descanso* for him.

Symbiotic Living

We'll close this conifer discussion with some practical care experience. New transplants here need very frequent water, then after several months, at least a monthly soak, even during the winter. As the roots grow laterally and shallowly, not down and deep, water them in a furrow at the drip line, not the trunk.

Besides root water, monitor the effects of local drought conditions on internal moisture level. Drought reduces the water content of trees from the usual 40 percent down to 15 percent, creating a higher fire risk.

The well around the tree should be mulched to a depth of several inches with organic material such as wood chips, compost, cotton burr material, or leaves. We believe this reproduces the wild forest floor duff. But leave about a foot space from the trunk to avoid fungal contamination. And Taos arborist Paul Bryan Jones says conifers breathe at their trunk base.

Watch the apex growth point, also called the terminal bud, that enables the trunk stem to grow longer. If damaged by birds or dry wind, prune it off to prevent destructive insect invasion. In general, a healthy tree will defend itself. Deadwood pruning can be done any time of year, but live branch shape pruning should be done only in the late winter when the tree is dormant.

The most harmful risk our trees have experienced is rodents such as prairie dogs and pocket gophers that tunnel in the root ball and love eating the new growth. Controlling them is another long discussion.

If you have at least an acre and want to do restoration planting, the New Mexico Energy, Minerals, and Natural Resources Department's Forestry Division conducts a Conservation Seedling Program. In 2021, sixty species were available at low cost. See www.emnrd.state.nm.us/SFD/.

However, do not despair if your planting survival disappoints. Soon after Aldo Leopold bought eighty acres of Sand County, Wisconsin, depleted farmland, according to biographer Meine,

> Leopold and his sons toyed with the idea of building a little forest for themselves. He ordered a thousand white pines and a thousand red pines from a nursery in Madison. Aldo hired a neighbor farmer to plow some furrows in the sandy soil. That spring was one of the driest on record and in summer, still no rain fell. His record of tree mortality: Norway pines 95% dead, Whites 99% dead, Mt. Ash 100% dead, Tamaracks 50% dead. They tried again the following spring.

However, eighty years later mature trees were harvested to build the new education building on the property, now the home of the national Aldo Leopold Foundation.

Leafy Friends

There are qualities and opportunities for companion-
ship with deciduous trees
also. Our bedroom has a
large window facing east
towards the 12,600-foot
Lake Fork Ridge, part of the
Wheeler Peak Wilderness at
the edge of Taos Ski Valley.
The day/night temperature
difference can range from
30 to 50 degrees, whether
the high is winter 35 or summer 95. Annette wondered,
wouldn't a deciduous tree
outside the window be good
for warming sun in winter

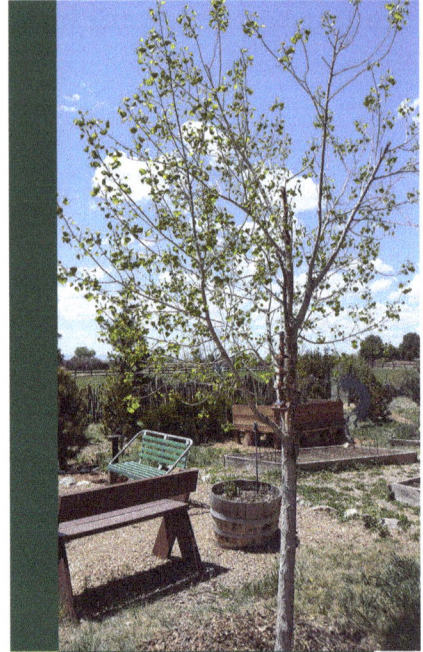

Early Leafing

and cooling shade in summer? Considering appearance, hardiness, commercial availability, and absence of noxious qualities, we chose thornless honey locust. Carter lists this as *Gle-
ditsia triacanthos*, a native to central North America. How is
this Rewilding? It is a tree adding to our biosphere, growing
well after seven years, and appreciated for its qualities.

One technical care issue with deciduous trees facing east, the
thin bark is vulnerable to frost burn. That occurs when late
winter warming sun stirs the tree out of dormancy. But the
flow of sap is frozen by later nocturnal cold and splits the
bark. The prevention is wrapping the trunk in burlap in No-
vember to insulate, then removing in April. Sounds like cooperative care to us. Rewilding does not exclude some stewardship.

Annette also sought leafy shade on the west house side to block strong afternoon sun on the patio. We decided to plant native Rio Grande cottonwoods, *Populous deltoides,* available in twelve to eighteen foot heights. They require moisture, so we installed roof water catchment barrels to supply them. Their expressive cycles of spring budding, summer leafing, autumn color turn, and winter shedding are appreciated in our home vista. The small birds, like chickadees and finches, welcome winter perching in the leafless branches.

Thinking further about deciduous tree adoptions, I have come to know Gambel oak, *Quercus gambelii,* that surround the Leopold Mi Casita in Tres Piedras. This scrub oak is ubiquitous in the southern Rockies. Finding them commercially available, albeit small, we now have ten filling in our front perimeter. While we confess to being limited in ornithological knowledge, the more trees we plant, the more birds of various types seem to enjoy the habitat additions year-round. More on this in Chapter 4.

One final practical resource. The Town of Taos Planning Office authorized creation of a Tree Board. Their program includes recognition of Heritage Trees. Their guide also has a thoughtful discussion of Siberian elms, *Ulmis pumila.* These were erroneously planted in the 1950s to green up the town, instead of the more desirable Chinese elms. Now our town wild Siberians are aggressive, invade rapidly, spread messy seedpods in pedestrian areas, and destroy underground utility pipes. However, they are also xeroscapic, meaning they will survive droughts and global warming better than other species. Yes, wild outcomes can surprise our predictions.

We add to this chapter another anecdote about living in community with conifers. Fifteen years ago, our home *après*-ski hot tub sat on the open front patio with a superb mountain view. Anyone like Alpenglow? For a screen from the neighbors, we bought five six-foot tall Wichita blue junipers living in pots. We classify these as compatible imports. Being sterile males, they do not produce pollen; junipers are notorious here for spring allergies. When we settled in the house full time, the hot tub was moved to the rear patio. We then planted the five trees down the backyard slope, a few feet apart in the small prairie grass area. Liberated from their pots, they are growing well. And a principle is endorsed, that trees like freedom to be rooted in the ground with their friends.

Gratitude for Trees

Reflecting on the Abrahamic dominion issue, we believe the teaching that privileged peoples' morality depends on practicing the difference between entitlement and gratitude. Friend Jenny Bird, Music Director at Unity of Taos, shared this song "Holy Trees."

> For the wood of our instruments, our shelters and
>   homes,
> Every fruit and nut that you bear.
> For the smell of new unfurled leaves,
> Soil of rotten leaves.
> Indeed for the whispering air that we breathe.
> To thee, oh to thee, hail oh holy tree.
> For the fire that warms our hearths,
> The cool of your shade.
> For the use of this table and chair.
> For the glory of autumn leaves,
> Medicines that you've made,
> Indeed for the whispering air that we breathe.
> To thee, oh to thee, hail holy tree.
> And the hillside remains a hillside
> With your roots sunk deep in the earth.
> And the stream gurgles sweet and clean

With the song your branches sing.
For the homes of many birds, creatures and
　crawling ones,
And all of the life you sustain.
For ships that sail the seas, paper and books we read,
Indeed for every breath we breathe.
To thee, oh to thee, Hail oh holy tree.
We're grateful to thee. Hail oh holy tree.

Trying to be true to our guides, an opportunity occurred for expressing John Tallmadge's practices of attentiveness and witness. Jenny Bird arranged for Taos friend Jenna Paulden to speak at a Unity Community service. She is a member of the Order of Bards, Ovates, and Druids, and shared a recent guidance from *The Celtic Spirit* by Caitlin Matthews on arboreal consciousness connections from our five human senses:

Sight-Insight,
Hearing-Resonance,
Taste-Discrimination,
Smell-Intuition,
Touch-Empathy.

As our goal is enhancing the process of relationship, we think of these human skills as alternatives to the practices of dominion power.

Rewilding with Horticulture and Husbandry

3 ✪

There is hardly an acre that does not tell its own story to those who understand the speech of hills and rivers."   Aldo Leopold, *The Virgin Southwest*, 1927.

We are writing for the many people wanting to Rewild in small, personal spaces. There have been several complex, thoughtful, creative systems and programs devoted to progressive agriculture, sometimes called ecoculture. An excellent comprehensive reference is Lisa Rayner's *Growing Food in the Southwest Mountains,* 2013. She includes this description from *The Permaculture Designer's Manual* by co-founder Bill Mollison:

> The conscious design and maintenance of agriculturally productive ecosystems is the harmonious integration of landscape and people providing their food, energy, shelter, and other material and non-material needs in a sustainable way.

While intriguing and inspirational as a Rewilding system, we have found rigorous permaculture more complex than we can do in our small space. Some commentators have simplified the experience of permaculture from its systematic procedures to awareness of ethical relationship with the Earth and alliance with natural processes. Rayner describes wild ecosystems as "gardens created by the interactions and coevolution of many species."

We interpret this Leopold view broadly to include the entire ecosphere, not just topography. We remark again that this little book is not about what you can and should do, but rather what we have done and the outcomes. How then can we hear and cultivate the stories on our small southwestern landscape? What can we do to accomplish the goals of fertility and habitat? That is why we choose the smaller term *horticulture* for cultivating gardens, orchards, and nurseries, rather than farming agriculture. To expand our values, the term *husbandry* offers multiple definitions. Beyond production of crops and animals for food, my thick dictionary states "frugal management of resources, as in conservation."

Attending to the Soil

Our depleted homescape land was 90 percent clay, judging by the sediment settling out in a jar of water. This is even too much clay for making adobe bricks that require about 40 percent sand and 10 percent organic matter. The straw organic component is notorious in the biblical story of making bricks in ancient Egypt (Exodus). Local New Mexico lore includes some burro manure also. Desiring much diversity in our plantings, we thought about differences in soil content. The native conifers described in Chapter 2 have done well in this soil without augmentation. However, following the advice of an arborist, we added about 25 percent acidic compost, such as organic cotton burr, to the hybrid pines' holes at plant-ing. This contributes both humus qualities and pH balance. Speaking of soil chemistry, we learned in the Taos County Master Gardener class that soil analysis is done by the Colorado State University Extension Service for thirty dollars. Results are provided for pH, texture, organic material, nitrate, phosphorous, potassium, zinc, iron, manganese, copper, boron, and gypsum. We have not used all that data, but it is interesting for an old doctor and science teacher to know. Tubes for mailing the sample to your state's ag school are likely available at the local county extension agent office.

Our Planting Wishes

Besides trees, we planned for garden vegetables, tomatoes, squash, sugar pumpkins, and beans; as many native flowers and shrubs as we could fit; and a fifty-foot diameter corn patch. The soil needs of these groups differ. As you walk around, the slope west down from the flagstone patio has been transformed into a rock garden now filled with flowering native forbs. There are two sections on the north and south sides of steps down from the patio, twenty feet wide and sloping eight feet to the west. The top border along a low adobe wall has ten Apache plume bushes, *Fallugia paradoxa*, and ten Wood's rose shrubs, *Rosa woodsia*, both natives. They are all happy getting roof runoff water, which we also capture in gutter pipe barrels for dry spells, so these are moderately well hydrated and drained beds. We have not augmented this soil, but each new planting gets a dose of organic fertilizer mix in the hole.

It is fun to cruise the nurseries and catalogs seeking additions to the native forb collection. We try to plant in trios when we can. Over the past ten years we have filled the space with red osier dogwood, *Cornus sericea;* creeping mahonia, *Ber-*

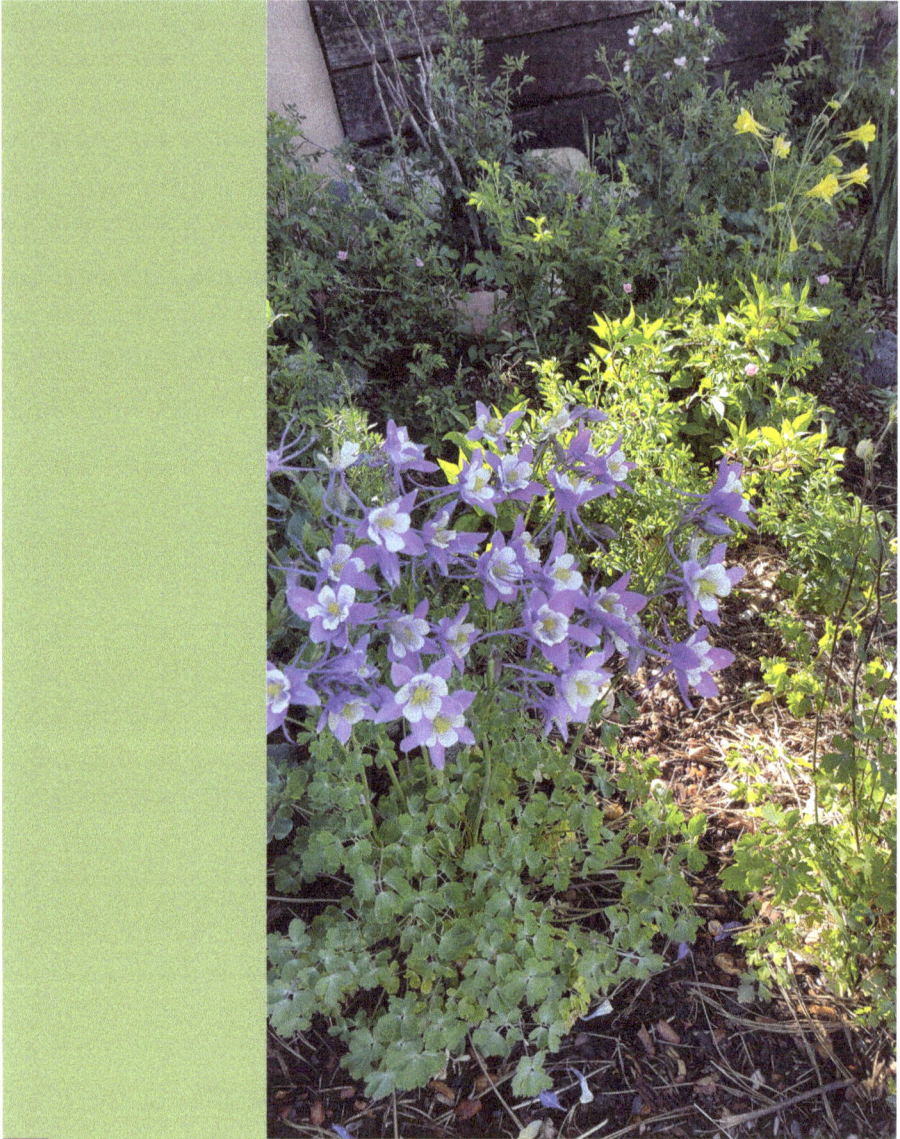

Columbines

beris repens; Colorado blue columbine, *Aquilegia caerulea*; golden columbine, *A. chrysantha*; Rocky Mountain bee plant, *Cleome serulata*; showy fleabane, *Erigeron speciosus*; Rocky Mountain iris, *Iris missouriensis;* western blue flax, *Linum*

lewisii; Colorado four o'clock, *Mirabilis multiflora;* berga-
mot beebalm, *Monarda fistulosa;* scarlet bugler, *Penstemon
barbatus;* Pineleaf penstemon, *P. pinifolius*; Rocky Mountain penstemon, *P. strictus;* purple aster, *Machaeranthera ca-
nescens;* scarlet globemallow, *Sphaeralcea angustifolia;* blue
sage, *Salvia azurea*; spike verbena, *V. macdougalii*; and wild
hyssop, *Agastache cana.*

We are depending on the guidebook *Native Gardening in
Northern New Mexico* by Sally Wasowski for the scientific
and common names. My Native Plant Society friends have
persuaded us to respect them, despite resistance from many
years of medical overexposure. A "Gnomenclature" wag in
the Taos Farm and Garden Facebook group described her
Plantus forgetticus and *Purchasum impulsii.* Over several
seasons, some of our plants have not survived, and some have
vigorously spread. One wilding strategy is to choose season blooming differences to nurture various pollinators. This
also expands the time for our pleasure of blooms. We mulch
spring and fall with New Mexico pecan shell. Pardon mulch
geekiness, but this choice is physically good for water retention and weed suppression, locally sourced, organic, nontox-
ic, and aesthetically attractive. It is also popular with the mice
and magpies finding nut bits. Finally, we do not cut the plant
stems and seeds in fall but leave them as winter habitat, shel-
ter, and food for insects and birds.

The garden play season is not over when the blooms fade.
Native seed collecting is productive and satisfying. Many
guides are available for wild and cultivated collection methods, timing, handling, storage etc. One of our favorite practices is in midwinter after the seeds of annuals like Rocky
Mountain bee plant and perennials like Rocky Mountain penstemon have had a cold stratification exposure on their stalks,
open half the pods and spread the seed. We leave some for re-

generation. The seeds will grow from the surface, not needing soil coverage. If you are collecting from natives in the wild, take no more than 10 percent to allow regeneration.

A Traditional Cultivation Endeavor

Despite my medical training in Latinate names, in this Rewilding context, I became concerned that our western taxonomy may colonize wildness. The names may be products of culture, not nature. They have a scientific purpose, but I see Rewilding value in greater awareness of plant names and their origins in relationship to humans. I realized caution about this when organizing the identification signs for the Millicent Rogers Museum garden. Here's an article I wrote for a Native American art exhibit there, subsequently published in the January, 2020, *New Mexico Native Plant Society Newsletter*:

> Many traditional Native and Hispanic artistic and cultural creations are derived from natural materials, for example, in devotional objects, weaving dyes, basket material, and pottery paint. The Millicent Rogers Museum protects and displays thousands of such heritage treasures, appreciated by Taoseños and visitors since 1956. The recent development of our native plant gardens expands understanding of the cultures and brings to life the formative art experiences. As I describe several garden exhibits, think about the ingenuity of these ancestors. Allow yourself to experience a closer relationship with these native plants that still have vitality for us, in both organized gardens and in the wild. In small ways, these experiences can help our fears of environmental destruction. Aldo Leopold had pioneering ecology experience in Arizona and New Mexico. As he articulated, when we take care not to dominate, we can live ethically in community with the land and all things.
>
> On entering the courtyard of Millicent Rogers Museum (MRM), you can see creeping mahonia, *Mahonia repens*; Rocky Mountain iris, *Iris missouriensis;* and big sagebrush, *Artemisia tridenta.* These plants produced yellow, brown, and

✪ Bee Plant

green dyes for early Rio Grande and Navajo weavings. The blooms of rabbit brush, *Ericameria nauseosa*, very common around our homes and fields, were also a source of textile dyes. See MRM Galleries 2 and 8 for early weaving exhibits. But sheep wool has natural oils that prevent dyeing, so skillful weavers used soapweed yucca, *Yucca glauca,* to first wash the wool. And while at it, the fronds yield excellent basket material. Looking carefully in Gallery 13, many Apache and Hopi yucca baskets have woven black designs. These come from the seed pods of devil's claw, *Proboscidea parviflora*, also known as *Martynia*. Growing wild in drier areas south of Taos, it was a common native trade item. After I had tried for three years to cultivate an example in the MRM gardens, one annual plant agreed to become an educational exhibit.

As we continue around the courtyard we come across blue flax, *Linum lewisii.* Flax was woven into linen; its flower made coloring dye. It is said that Cortez was amazed at the beautiful clothing worn by the Aztecs. Growing proudly in a courtyard tall pot (from the third generation of these seeds) Rocky Mountain bee plant, *Cleome serrulata,* has been used by Pueblo artisans to produce the black paint for polychrome pottery, as in Gallery 4. Not to overlook the shrubberies, red osier dogwood, *Cornus sericea,* grows here at the southern end of its range, and I'm told can be found high on Pueblo Peak. The Midwestern Potawatomi people created "dreamcatchers," using the flexible red stems for frames. Our local tribes similarly employed it in basketry. Last in this selective tour, the humble mountain mahogany, *Cercocarpus montanus,* produced a red dye used for early Navajo and Rio Grande weavings, but was soon replaced by stronger commercial, albeit still natural, trade dyes: East Indian indigo and Mesoamerican cochineal beetle extract. Consider this a living-learning experience exhibit. Now you can recognize them all around us, cultivate them yourselves, produce artful creations, and appreciate their qualities in our shared world.

Some of you may question our display of English and Latinate scientific names on the Native American and Hispanic traditional plants. From a social justice perspective, this

✪ Flax Going Wild

can be considered as domination colonizing. Why not Taos Pueblo *Tiwa* and *Norteño* Spanish? Former Director Caroline Fernald, PhD in Native American Art, advised that was not appropriate because there are different names among many native tribes, and some names are religiously secret.

Relationships of Wild and Native

Let's think about the comparison of native plants to wild ones. Some friends in the New Mexico Native Plant Society Taos Chapter are devoted to the idea of growing only natives. This is admirable practice and the identification activity in various environments can be fun. Excellent botany texts have been published, such as Robert DeWitt Ivey's *Flowering Plants of New Mexico.* We have the 2003 Fourth Edition. The ecological benefits are many for pollinators, diversity restoration, and soil nurture. Yet wild includes much more than native origins. The term *invasive* is applied to an accidental or deliberate plant intrusion, usually noxious. We leave to scholars the question of how long a plant is present before being classified as native. Russian sage, formerly *Perovskia atriplicifolia,* but since 2017, named *Salvia yangii,* is popular around Taos and extensively sold commercially. A small perennial shrub, it is native to Central Asia, particularly the Himalayas, and very hardy here in dry, alkaline soil. It is both pretty with many small blue flowers and attractive to pollinators. We often see bumblebees and hummingbirds visiting the dozen plants on the east side of our house. We can't think of a negative feature, so consider this immigrant now naturalized.

Here's another domestic-to-wild plant evolution story from the Leopold cabin. Cruising around the area doing odd jobs a few years ago after a wet winter, a friend pointed out a humble patch of unusual greenery at the front southeast corner saying, "That looks like hops." Not a familiar plant, I did some identification study. Southern Methodist University

Botany Professor John Ubelaker, now retired in Taos, said it could be a type of hops, but the native species, *Humulus lupulis,* is rare here. Having lunch at the Chili Line Depot Café across the road, I often swapped stories with Sheila Roberts, a third-generation Tres Piedras local. Her great grandfather Walter Perry was foreman overseeing the building of the cabin for Leopold as well as his hunting buddy. Walter wrote a neat memoir about his Forest Service life. Out of print, Sheila gave me a copy for the Mi Casita library. She said that the old Anglo settlers here one hundred to one hundred fifty years ago grew European hops to make their own beer. I told our friend Greg from Carson who also grows his own, and he verified the identity. The location is below the roof overhang corner, and surely the seeds were dropped by a local avian having lunch. We have pulled some crowding cheat grass and provide water occasionally for this patch now rewilded.

One Northern New Mexico perennial flower, iconic in landscape paintings usually along an adobe wall, is hollyhock, *Alcea rosea.* They have been traditional here for so long, we may think they are native. Their origin is East Asia, and Europeans first encountered them in the Crusades. Leonardo Ortiz, a *Hermano* from Arroyo Hondo who was maintenance engineer at the Millicent Rogers Museum, told me the legend of an itinerant Franciscan, subsequently named St. Joseph. He was looking for chapel sites in Iberia and stayed overnight at a humble inn, leaving his staff outside the door. In the morning, the staff had become a beautiful flowering hollyhock. The Franciscans honored this holy sign and brought hollyhocks to New Spain for planting at chapels and churches. And as nature is wonderfully diverse, or at least humans' taxonomies, there is a different true native flower in the Sandia mountains called wild hollyhock, *Iliamna grandiflora.*

Planting for pollinators, especially hummingbirds, is popular now. Here is a sweet story that combines wild gardening with Leopold's interest in peoples' relationship to each other and to the land. Annette made friends with Marcie Coulter from Kentucky in the Taos Master Gardener class. When Annette needed some surgery, Marcie gave her a get well smile of seeds for two dozen hummer attraction flowers. We have a delightful season here from April to September of broad-tails and rufous visiting our syrup feeders. And they like our red *Penstemon barbatus* and the blue Russian sage. While deciding where to plant these seeds, we thought of Leopold's wisdom. The guidance: make friends with the people who will join you in Rewilding, people aware of our relationship to the land.

Understanding Weeds

Besides local longevity, plants' qualities affect their fate with humans. The NM State College of Agricultural, Consumer, and Environmental Sciences Cooperative Extension Service published a guidebook in 2010: *Troublesome Weeds of New Mexico.* A weed has been defined as a plant undesirable in a particular situation, as in the wrong place. From his transcendentalist view, Ralph Waldo Emerson famously said, "A weed is a plant whose virtues have not yet been discovered." Evolutionary biologists believe weeds developed in the early days of human plant gathering, then increased with Neolithic early agriculture soil disturbance 12,000 years ago.

Note that the judgment of weediness is dependent on context. Some may be welcome as *volunteer* plants. Let's pause here and recognize the qualities of plants we call volunteer. These are defined as growing on their own, not deliberately planted. The usual distinction from weeds is their desirability, not rejection. Note the value judgment. Thinking about that dis-

✿ Volunteer Wild Rose

tinction, we wonder what empowers some seeds to become volunteers? To survive and assert themselves? To live long and prosper? (Sorry, Spock.) When volunteers sprout in our various gardens, even though possibly "out of place," we admire and nurture them. In addition to natural vectors, such as birds and wind, our worm compost feedings sometimes introduce volunteer seeds as well. A cantaloupe plant, not a typical member of our garden family, once started in the rhubarb bed. Botanists sometimes discover new cultivars that way. In our garden relationships, we welcome volunteers as new wilder friends.

Another criterion for defining weed harm is aggressive growth that obliterates other plants. *The Troublesome Weeds of New Mexico* guide states:

Weeds have been documented to cause displacement of native plants and animals, increased fire danger, increased soil erosion, increased flood severity, increased soil salinity, and decreased water quality.

The issues are far more extensive than the dandelions in your lawn. We pursue the topic because so-called weeds are prominent in our relationship with wildness. The guidebook describes four categories. The twenty-one Class A species were not present in New Mexico as of 2010 or have limited distribution; preventing new infestations and eradicating existing plants are of highest priority. The ten Class B species are limited to portions of the state; our management should contain the infestation and prevent further spread. The six Class C are widespread; management at the local level should be based on feasibility of control and the amount of infestation. Very familiar around Taos, they are bull thistle, cheatgrass, jointed goatgrass, Russian olive, saltcedar, and Siberian elm. In addition, eight species are in a Watch List category, of concern in the state with the potential to become problematic.

Ubiquitous common dandelions, *Taraxacum erythrospermum,* are not on these lists and have an interesting story, told to me by Professor John Ubelaker. The Romans included apothecaries in their military expeditions. Dandelions were native to the Balkans and the stem sap was found to have blood coagulant properties, helpful for wound treatment. Therefore, their use in the pharmacopeia of invading armies spread the plant extensively. Spanish conquistadors likely brought them to New Mexico.

Another plant in ambiguous relationship is bindweed. An invasive from Europe, it is the same species as the popular morning glory, *Convolvulus arvensis.* It is a ground creeper with one inch white flowers that will envelope other plants and form dense tangled mats. If your field has nothing else, it can be pretty greenery. But once in your garden beds, it is a devil to get rid of. As Annette's Master Gardener friend (also an accountant) Marcie says, "Sure things in life are death, taxes, and bindweed."

Continuing around the periphery inside our home *latilla* fence, we transplanted Maximilian sunflowers, *Helianthus maximiliani,* to behind the conifers on the south side. These are vigorous natives of mid- and southern Rio Grande riparian wetlands. Once established, they grow up to six feet tall, propagate many shoots, and yield hundreds of yellow blooms in early fall. The birds love the many small seeds over winter. The long stalks provide habitat for insects that entomologists call *pithy stem nesters*. In early spring, we cut the stalks down to a few inches, making room for the many new shoots. Moderate watering helps their vigor. We gifted a bucket full of rooted stems to work-in-progress homescapers. The transplants sprouted and bloomed the next season. This is a very dynamic plant when allowed to be wild!

Living in Cultivation

Moving further counterclockwise, in front of little *Kokopelli's* teepee, we have a mix of perennial purple coneflowers, *Echinacea angustifolia,* mixed with our native showy milkweed, *Asclepias speciosa*. While this milkweed grows vigorously in local roadside ditches, deliberate propagation has been difficult for me. Though unsuccessful propagating them from seeds, we have established several plants as starts obtained from High Country Gardens native nursery in Santa Fe. Unfortunately, we have yet to see any monarch butterflies attracted.

A few steps toward the yard center, two wooden half barrels have become favorite places for a historic plant addition, Rocky Mountain bee plant, *Cleome serrulata*. This is an annual that reseeds itself and grows wild along high mountain dirt roads where soil has been disturbed. The three-foot shoots with bunches of small bluish flowers have been collected and cultivated for centuries by the middle Rio Grande Pueblos because the entire plant yields a brown paint when boiled. Used for designs on white pottery, when fired, the paint turns black, making polychrome pots. We have one from Acoma, received in trade for a horse bridle in 1975. The seed pods can be collected easily when dry in the fall. Here's an indicator your practice and attitude are going wild: your bee plant seeds have blown around and germinate profusely. We have them coming up in the pumpkin patch, on the crusher fine steps below the *horno*, and in fire pit gravel. Of course, we leave them to flourish wildly.

From long before modern Pueblo crafts, the black designs (often distinctive signatures of tribes) identify pottery sources made as trade items in Precontact times. I went beyond being just a student of this process by boiling late summer plants for twenty-four hours to yield the brown liquid. Not having pottery to paint and fire, I decided to reproduce a personal image on a pueblo drum skin. This was a "grandfather tree" amulet received in the New Mexico Men's Wellness group Elder ceremony a decade ago.

Surveying our Foodscape

In the yard's center, we have built four raised beds, or more accurately, eight-by-eight foot beds contained within ten-inch boards. These are filled with soil developed for specialized vegetable growing. They are rich in compost for good water retention and nurture of the many tiny creatures that keep our planet's biota alive. Some practices we do from traditional knowledge, as in our childhood family Victory Gardens, to foster earthworms and beneficial insects. In addition, we have also learned much from Lowenfels and Lewis's 2010 *Teaming with Microbes*. Let's be grateful for our wild nematodes, fungi, and bacteria, to mention a few usually unseen garden helpers. Yet these, too, need cultivation of their wildness, providing them their own foods, nutrients, and water.

Going macroscopic, we fortify the bed soils with nitrogen and needed elements from a red wriggler worm, *Eisenia fetida,* compost bin. This "ranch" is built of straw bales and topsoil is regularly added as we remove matrix with the castings for garden plant nourishment. It has been productive for six years, fed with our kitchen vegetable refuse. While I do insulate them over the winter with several inches of straw and a tarp cover for survival, each spring we import another herd for the ranch from commercial suppliers. Whether we consider the worms domesticated or wild, most choose this feedlot habitat, providing us a more natural fertilizer method than buying industrial products.

On the topic of animal community, the garden bed plants are helped by useful insects, such as lacewings, ladybugs, and praying mantis that feed on destructive aphids. Annette regularly adds to our homescape population, particularly to defend her tomato plants. The ladybugs are very independent. When woken from dormancy in the refrigerator and spread on the tomato plants, they tend to love our feast for a night, then leave. Watching tiny praying mantis hatch from the egg cases she buys is fascinating. They disappear camouflaged in the garden, but occasionally we find a large one weeks later. And there is a better purpose for spiders inside your home's nooks and crannies. Catch them in a cup and relocate to the garden beds.

We are selective in our garden crops, focusing on tomatoes, peas, carrots, red beans, eggplants, cucumbers, rhubarb, acorn

✿ Tending Tomatoes

squash, and small pie pumpkins. While permaculture encourages perennial plants, we do favor several annuals for cuisine and growing pleasure. We try to practice selective companion planting. Some seem to thrive simply out of proximity, some share nutrients such as nitrogen fixing legumes, and some repel destructive insects. Annette likes large blossom marigolds around the tomatoes to ward off aphids, and they are also pretty. Adding some basil, scallions, dill, nasturtiums, and radishes, we have diverse companion beds. While we do pull invasives like cheatgrass and bindweed in the garden beds, we also protect spaces with straw. Nope, no toxic insect or weed killers.

While thinking of soil augmentation, we offer a few words here on our manure experience. The freely available horse road apples are not advised. Their digestion passes through many weed seeds. Sheep and cow forage is digested hotter and less seed prolific. However, fresh of any kind can burn plants. Better to mix it in your brown compost pile. Another restoration adjustment that helps wild creatures is avoidance of the popular solar path lights. While appearing attractive, we have decided they disrupt the natural life of nocturnal insects.

One beloved crop, more accurately called ancient domesticated rather than wild, is Pueblo blue corn, properly known

✺ Early Blue Corn Patch and Corn Maiden

as maize. We devoted a chapter in the *Taos Horno Adventures* book to the blessings of our labyrinth patch. This story was posted recently on the Taos Farm and Garden Facebook group, source unknown:

> There was a farmer who grew excellent quality corn. Every year he won the award for the best grown corn. One year a newspaper reporter interviewed him and learned something interesting about how he grew it. The reporter discovered that the farmer shared his seed corn with his neighbors. "How can you afford to share your best seed corn with your neighbors when they are your competitors?" the reporter asked. "Why sir," said the farmer, "Didn't you know? The wind picks up pollen from the ripening corn and swirls it from field to field. If my neighbors grow inferior corn, cross-pollination will steadily degrade the quality of my corn. If I am to grow good corn, I must help my neighbors grow good corn.
>
> So it is with our lives. Those who want to live meaningfully and well must help enrich the lives of others, for the value of a life is measured by the lives it touches. And those who choose to be happy must help others find happiness, for the welfare of each is bound up with the welfare of all.

We see social justice in this wild practice. We also find expression of ecocentric values as plants like Pueblo blue corn are considered sacred by many tribes, particularly the pollen. While avoiding Native American imitation and cultural appropriation, we can admire the human-biosphere relationship. We have intentionally practiced traditions of our own historic culture with the corn. As early Hebrew tribes had many pastoral practices, our spring planting blessing includes Annette leading the women in providing water as Miriam did during the Exodus. Since this story is one of many spiritual transformations occurring in a **wild**erness, I wonder if this practice qualifies as Re**wild**ing.

Our husbandry conservation practices can include technology. Not fortunate to be an *acequia parciente,* and not wanting

Fall Blue Corn Patch

to stress our home's moderate well, we installed a 1,700-gallon roof rainwater and snow melt catchment tank. It is buried so as not to freeze and, with its own pump driven off my rooftop solar system, I can run hoses to garden beds, regulated in balance with natural precipitation. Specific beds may vary in their water needs; rhubarb and pumpkins, for example, require more water than Pueblo red beans. Many people like to put their drip systems on timers. We do not, because we are the best regulators of when different beds and plant types need water in their growth process with natural dynamics. In other words, we do not defer to tubes and clocks what we can do with visits often to our garden companions. Our favorite watering measurement tool is digital. (Think about that.) In our small-scale place, this helps us have more kincentric relationship with the plants.

A Native Shrubberetum

As we continue this survey clockwise around our garden land periphery to the north, we established a row of native shrubbery inside the *latilla* fence, curious to know many new plants and learn from them. And we saw value in providing diverse menus and habitats for various nonhuman life. We recommend a thin but rich guide, *Native Gardening in Northern New Mexico,* by Sally Wasowski, available through the Native Plant Society of New Mexico. Moving along on our tour, we encounter chokecherry, *Prunus virginiana;* Apache plume, *Fallugia paradoxa;* mountain mahogany, *Cercocarpus montanus;* three-leaf sumac, *Rhus trilobata;* golden currant, *Ribes aureum;* fernbush, *Chamaebatiaria millefolium;* and another Apache plume. Looking over the fence, one can see Utah serviceberry, *Amelanchier utahensis;* big sagebrush, *Artemisia tridentata; and* chamisa (rabbitbrush), *Ericameria nauseosa.* Turning toward the inner yard, we added Arizona honeysuckle, *Lonicera arizonica;* red osier dogwood, *Cornus sericea;* Woods' rose, *Rosa woodsia;* wild plum, *Prunus americana;* and three new littleleaf mockorange, *Philadelphus microphyllus.* We cannot claim a complete shrubberetum according to Wasowski's catalog, but are glad for these.

We have been successful establishing the New Mexico native milkweed, *Asclepias speciosa,* in the north and south border areas. It is desirable for the monarch butterflies who used to travel from wintering in the Mexico Sierra Madre Mountains to summer breeding throughout North America. I saw many as a kid in the fields of Cape Cod and the Adirondacks many decades ago. A marvelous film of the Monarch life cycle was inspiring. However, the population has severely diminished, and pesticides are blamed. We have not seen a Monarch here for several years. Tiger swallowtails are the common large

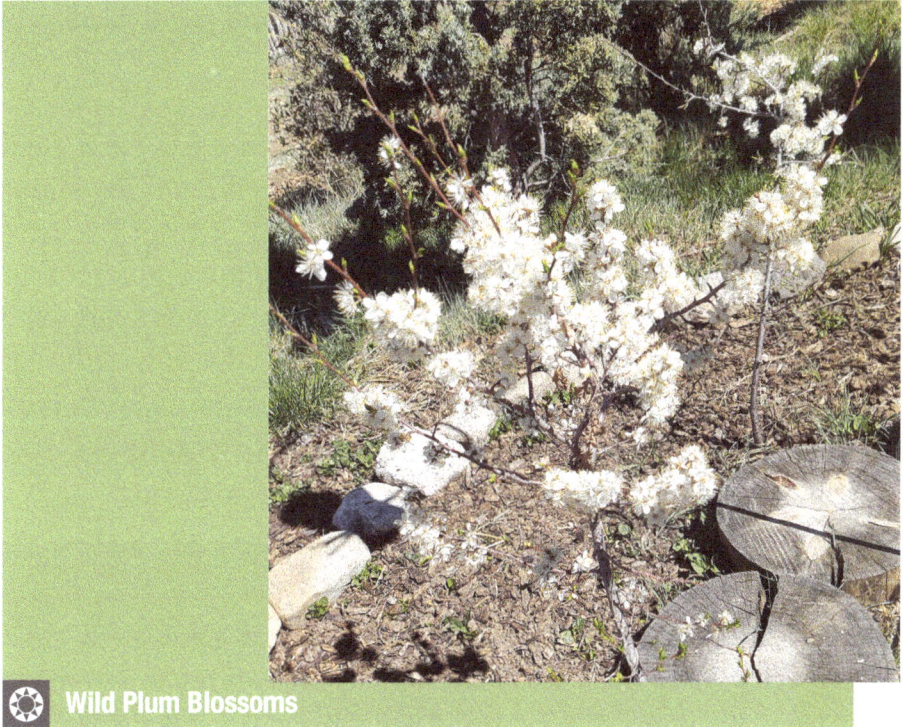

❂ Wild Plum Blossoms

butterfly. Yet the showy milkweeds are valuable pollinators and habitat for many other species.

While showy milkweed grows wild in the ditches along small roads here, the propagation at home was not easy. However, this story shows what can be accomplished by restoration Rewilding persistence. As a first consideration, seed pods are freely available to collect along the roads. These have lovely tufts that catch the autumn breezes. We began with such local seeds, covered them with burlap to protect from the magpies, and kept them moist. After no germination, the next season I tried commercial seeds, but again to no avail. Moving on in the search for resources, we turned to High Country Gardens, which has been a reliable and authentic source of native plant starts. Their extensive catalogs are very educational. I ordered a half dozen *Asclepias*; four were planted among the north border fence shrubs and two in the south diverse bed mixed with established globe mallow and coneflowers. All survived transplanting, and some produced typical pink flower bunches and seed pods the first year. We left the stalks through the winter, then cut to ground early spring. Patience is a virtue. The original six plants have become eighteen four years later, and they deserve to be honored now as wild. And it is good to trust the seeds' wildness. I spread some in the Mi Casita native garden three years ago. This June I discovered several new sprouts. We'll water them often this summer for a rooting boost, and hopefully some flowers next year.

As we have walked you around the periphery of our home's west side one third acre, consider the center next. The south third is a gravel circle with a fire pit in the shape of a Zia sun symbol. Helping a widow friend needing to move out of state, we got it in trade for two mountain bikes for her grandchildren. We were getting too old for them anyway. Let's add a cultural respect comment about the ubiquitous New Mexico Zia Pueblo insignia. The tribe has recently pursued appropriate compensation for the commercial use of their intellectual property. The firepit frame was made by a local metal artist for personal use. And just for fun, around the pit we put two old Taos Ski Valley lift chairs on logs. They were sold when a ski lift was replaced, and the money was sent to hurricane relief in east Texas. I also built two reproductions of Leopold benches. This is a simple design Aldo made for the family's outdoor living at its Wisconsin Shack. Plans can be obtained from the Leopold Foundation. These objects with historic stories inform our consciousness.

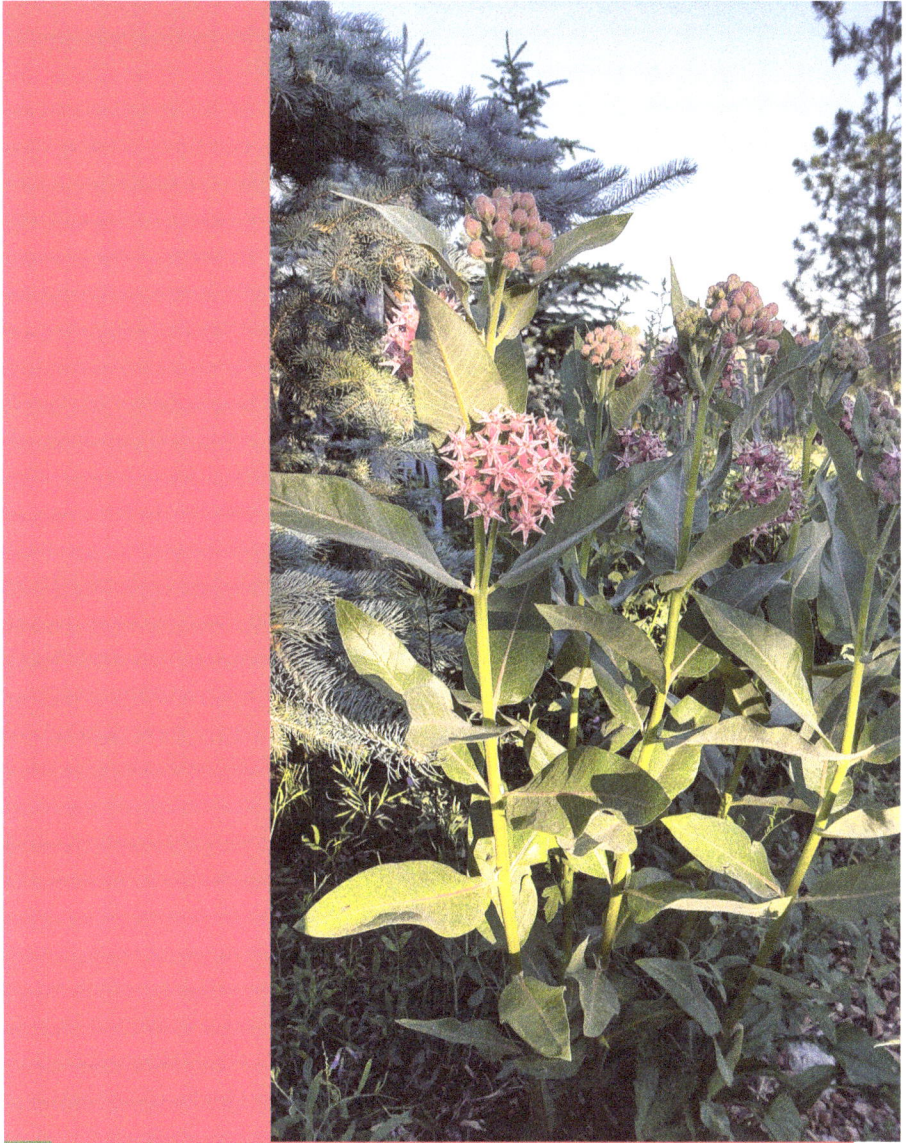

✿ Showy Milkweed

A Small Wild Prairie

The yard midcenter is devoted to a quartet of raised garden beds. And the north third has another wild habitat, a small prairie of various native grasses. Yes, a small wild area consisting of sideoats grama, *Bouteloua curtipendula;* blue grama, *Bouteloua gracilis*; fringed brome, *Bromus ciliatus*; mountain muhly, *Muhlenbergia montana;* muttongrass *Poa fendleriana;* and Indian ricegrass, *Oryzopsis hymenoides.* Native prairie grass mixtures are available from regional commercial sources. One quality of the mix is different species' blooming at various season times. We are creating habitat, creature food, soil nurture, and wild appearance. To establish, warmer soil is best, over fifty degrees. Scratch but not plow the soil, spread seed, and add a thin layer of fine compost such as mushroom. To prevent the seeds becoming a smorgasbord for the birds, cover with burlap. The mice will get some, hopefully just a tithe. Water daily the first month until shoots poke through, then remove the burlap and water if your rainy season, here called monsoons, has not started. Two years of seeding may be needed for perennial establishment. Never mow or fertilize; let it accommodate to be wild. I do use a rechargeable electric string trimmer to spread seeds in the spring and discourage intrusive bully plants.

Seeds of chamisa, cheatgrass, and alfalfa will blow in. There are two species of alfalfa common here. The blue flowered variety, *Medicago sativa,* is the popular commercial feed hay crop, originally from ancient Persia, then brought into Europe. A similar yellow flowered plant is sweet clover, *Melilotus officinalis*, from Eurasia that has been introduced worldwide. It was originally used as a cover crop for soil improvement and is a valuable pollinator for honeybees. These plants are nitrogen fixers, so we leave some in balance with the grasses. Certain natives will also find the undisturbed field, such as spike verbena, *Verbena macdougalii*; prairie cone flower, *Ratibida columnifera;* and American vetch, *Vicia americana,* all welcome. And please pause often to experience what this wild prairie communicates to you through the changing seasons.

Beauty is also Truth

Rewilding does not require scruffiness. Some areas of the east house front land are seeded with diverse native wildflowers. These are aesthetic, pollinator nutritive, and various creature beneficial; they also block invasive weeds and firm muddy clay. We are definitely opposed to conventional grass lawns. We have one ten by twenty foot area just below the native rock garden, made by high mowing native blue grama grass to fill the space with lateral roots and frequent watering off gutter collection barrels. Less mud for grandkids and puppies.

You can be decorative with Rewilding. Along a part of the house front wall, Annette maintains a bed of perennial *Gaillardia pulchella,* also known as Indian blanket flower. These natives can be bought at local nurseries. The Taos Native Plant Society chapter does sales of their greenhouse cultivation. The *Gaillardia* produce numerous seeds. We will not detail methods for planting native flower seeds. Good information is available fitting your growing zone and sowing season depending on species' choice. No land should be bare of wild value plants. If you are interested in collecting wild seeds, consult your local native plant society. The Taos group has an informative website. The Wildones.org program offers native plant garden designs for several eastern and Midwest states. Douglas Tallamy's 2019 *Nature's Best Hope* has thorough and constructive descriptions of restoration conservation for urban and suburban yards, with East Coast emphasis.

Rewilding does not require athletic strength and stamina. Resilience and balance are necessary human physical goals. In our senior years, we added a ramp from the rear patio and workshop to the garden a few feet lower downslope. As Annette became troubled more by lower back arthritis while tending her tomato plants, I built her a raised bed at standing waist height. While a pretty good gardener, I'm not a structural engineer. Eighteen inches of wet soil are heavy. Douglas fir stump rounds bought from Olquin's sawmill support the belly. We are reminded of farmer-poet Wendell Berry's description of a nurturer's ethics. The goal is health: of one's land, one's own, one's family, one's community, one's planet.

Annette has a favorite indoor Rewilding experience. Twenty years ago, attending a parents' weekend with our daughter at Bates College in Maine, we adopted a struggling *Dieffenbachia* plant when touring the campus greenhouse. About eighteen inches tall, it was maybe the result of a student flunking their botany class. Yes, this was a plant rescue. *Dieffenbachia seguine* is native to Central and South American tropics. We observed them as thick shrubs on a trip to Costa Rica. However, this plant really likes Annette and its life with us, first in our Vermont home, and next in the Taos house. The original has had four progeny and is now grown to the nine-foot ceiling, needing several top leaf trimmings. As we write this, the force of its wildness continues; there are three new leaf buds emerging, and a new shoot grows from the pot soil. Even though living in domesticated conditions, this immigrant native outdoor plant continues to assert itself, and add to our **wilder**ness awareness.

Living as Fauna

4

We sally forth, the dog and I, at random. He has paid scant re-spect to all these vocal goings-on [bird songs], for to him the ev-idence of tenantry is not song, but scent. Any illiterate bundle of feathers, he says, can make a noise in a tree. Now he is going to translate for me the olfactory poems that who-knows-what silent creatures have written in the summer night. Aldo Leopold, *A Sand County Almanac,* 1949.

Leopold captures an engaging example of human and wilder-other relationship. A recent *Science* magazine ar-ticle described the qualities that made certain canines evolve differently and become prototypic dogs, possibly twenty thousand years ago. They learned to communicate and coop-erate with humans. Current dogs show these characteristics on a wide spectrum. Instead of rambling on about what our great companions do, observe your own canine, and maybe other homescape creatures that expand our consciousness of more than human wildness.

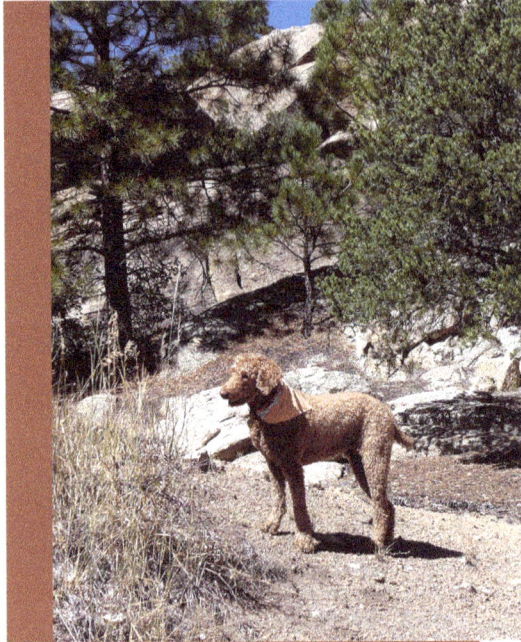

✿ **Translating Olfactory Poems**

Insect Citizens

While many are obvious, insects are much more ubiquitous than we see. It is popular to foster the pollinators such as hive bees, yet many solitary and ground dwelling bees are also important. A few years ago, we bought a commercial mason bee nesting box made of many small bamboo tubes. While interesting for us to look at, no one moved in. The *latilla* fencing described in Chapter 3 is made from young aspen poles, usually sold in eight-foot lengths. Friend Felipe is a contractor with a yard full of everything potentially useful, whenever. I obtained many *latillas* at a good price, some with interesting organic shapes. Our rear garden is protected by a four-foot pig wire fence attached to T posts. I used baling wire to attach sections of *latilla* on the inside for both traditional aesthetic appearance and windbreak, and even played with curving the top contour. In our warm dry weather, it was a meditative, methodical experience, so I call it our Zen fence. The *latillas* have many cracks that provide insect habitat. I have increased the nesting sites for mason bees by drilling holes in the posts. Annette and I also like the look of natural wood material, instead of metal or painted fence. It is also a visual barrier to the prairie dog residents of the neighbor's field. Yup, they are scouting forage as well as on guard for predators when standing up. Their Spanish name is expressive, *Ardillo ladradora*, "barking squirrels."

✦ First Swallowtail of the Season

The *latilla* fence also serves as garden windbreak. This is valuable for protecting various plants. Especially in the spring, the afternoon winds from the west can be intense. You can set a watch by their usual start at noon. Their regular and vigorous presence gives them a mythic character, like the Diablos or Mistrals. Here are a *Norteña* woman's words from Robert Coles' 1973 *The Old Ones of New Mexico*. I was privileged to hear him describe this work that year when a resident at the University of New Mexico Hospitals:

> The wind can be a friend or an enemy. A severe wind reminds us of our failures: something we forgot to fasten down. A gentle wind is company. I have to admit, I can spend a long time listening to the wind go through the trees and watching it sweep across the grass.

Snake Friends

Various wild plants grow at the fence base, often seeded by perching birds. The established vegetation, moisture, and insect diversity are favored by our resident garter snakes. One came out every morning last spring and summer from her nest in a south facing stacked beam terrace wall to warm up for about an hour. I once found her shed skin, and our eight-year-old grandson thought that was very cool. Judging by her thick abdomen and rapid taper to tail, she was a female in gestation. While we were eager to find her progeny sometime, she disappeared midsummer. But wild creatures can bring joyful surprises. The next June, a larger male appeared at the same wall's base. Maybe her mate?

This is a sweet example of community with a wild creature on their terms, not our domination. We have not seen other snake species. Tourists in the neighborhood sometimes ask about rattlesnakes. We don't have any at our 7,200-foot elevation, but they are common in the Rio Grande Gorge at about 6,000 feet. Occasionally neighbors with wetter lands along *acequias* will report bull snakes that are welcome for rodent control.

Marine Experience

Rachel Carson was very influential in my young environmental awareness which began in the 1950s at the Woods Hole Marine Biological Laboratory Childrens' Summer Science School at age nine or ten. Carson's 1951 *The Sea Around Us* was our handbook exploring the tide pools. My father had worked at the lab as a graduate student and later brought the family there summers.

Founded by the pioneering Harvard biologist Louis Agassiz, the lab's motto was "Study Nature, not Books." The story is told that he would sit his freshman biology students in front of a fish and direct them to describe all they see. There was also a spiritual inspiration for me at the MBL. A bronze Buddha stood in the lobby, and I would often check the statue's cupped hands because the scientists believed luck would grace their research when coins were left to delight children.

During these early learning years, I found intriguing the symbiosis concepts of parasitism, commensalism, and mutualism. To give common examples, do we drain our hosts of vitality like a tapeworm, do we live together cooperatively like ramora fish on sharks, or do we enhance life for each other, like clown fish and sea anemones? These distinctions are still important ecological attitudes for our Rewilding strategies.

Avian Community

In our Taos home yard, deliberate benefits for the birds are diverse trees, seed plants, shelters, water warmed in winter, suet, protection from predators, plant and garden beds with insect and vermiform food, ample seed stations, and seasonal nectar feeders. A recent *Science* magazine article reported that artificial seed feeders do not disrupt wild birds' habits and comprise only 30 percent of their diet when natural food is also available. Therefore, support the wild sources.

Winter Habitat

✿ **Hummingbird Sunset**

These provisions have brought us a couple dozen regular visitors; it is likely we would identify more if we were astute ornithologists. The little ones are apparently finches, towhees, sparrows, and in winter, chickadees. Colorful smiles are grosbeaks, woodpeckers, flickers, robins, and occasional goldfinches. Mountain bluebirds are rare. We enjoy the call of red-winged blackbirds from nearby cattail wetlands. On a May Day walkabout to survey for new spring sprouts and to water the carrot and radish seed bed, the western meadowlarks were particularly joyous among the surrounding plum tree blossoms. By noon, they rested.

Reviewing these names and realizing my avian fauna scientific nomenclature deficiency, I remembered a commentary that the human naming of creatures described in Genesis is an act of possessive domination. We may be imposing our views on their nature, rather than living with and learning from them. The use of human discoverer names suggests this also. There are alternatives where anthropologists, or better, indigenous observers, have organized comprehensive wild nomenclatures. As we become more open to natural process in our lives, knowing these is appealing. Orion magazine is dedicated to "People and Nature." A recent article described that South American biologist Carlos Morochz discovered an unnamed tree frog. Combining words from Ecuador's Kichwa, a local people of Inca descent, and Yumbo, a now-extinct tribe that once inhabited the Ecuador cloud forest, he created the name *mashpi* meaning "friend of the water."

Back to our homescape, special visitors are the broadtail and rufous hummingbirds, coming in late April and leaving in September unerringly before the first hard night frost. The male scouts find food sources that will support nearby nesting for their mate. And besides the nectar feeders, several summer native flowers are very popular with the hummers, such as red *Penstemon barbatus*.

Another example of our exercising a Rewilding consciousness was adapting a ten-foot peach tree in the west garden bed to the birds. When it did not survive a harsh spring, instead of cutting down, I did some pruning, and now it is our "peach perch." The petite hummers like the view from the top branches.

We must be doing something right with our seed feeders because a pair of mourning doves has adopted our territory. They sit on top of the pergola at the corn labyrinth entrance to catch the morning sun. They also love the seeds knocked off the hanging feeder above the rock garden. One early spring evening observing from the patio, I saw a single dove on the west *latilla* fence. Then a few minutes after another came, alighting close by. I heard cooing calls and watched the newcomer do a bowing dance. Then they both flew off together, likely for romance. Sweet. The couple were evident every day throughout spring. Then we observed only one around

Doves Catching Morning Sun

the yard, but the cooing from a tall Ponderosa was frequent. Some research explained that they announced their territory and the couple shares egg incubation shifts.

One morning, our puppy found a fledgling dove dead at the tree base. We then observed the pair out together around their favorite yard perches, and even seeming to nuzzle. Soon after, more cooing was heard from the adjacent tall Ponderosa. I saw one bird bringing straw pieces up high for a new nest. These creatures were showing resilience after a wild event affected their lives. A week later, a third adult dove appeared, and the trio often perched peacefully on the sunshine pergola. Why was this newcomer here? Maybe there are two nests in adjacent ponderosas? We are happy to provide them habitat at our homescape. Doves have represented much diverse symbolism in our human cultures and religions: Noah's Ark evidence of land, the Christian sign for the Messiah, and the classic Woodstock poster, to name a few instances.

Magpie Watching Us — Nesting Magpie Neighbor

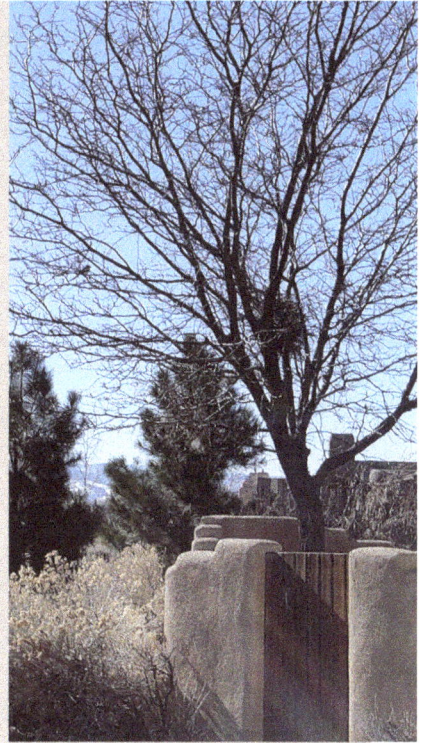

Our black-billed magpies are at the top of the seed feeder pecking order. They are handsome in black and white, long-tailed, acrobatic, intrusive, curious, smart, and noisy. They work in groups and a clutch will harass larger birds like hawks. The local Spanish name, *urraca*, is derived from a medieval Latin girl's name said belonging to princesses of Iberian Leon. One translation is "thievish" because legend has it that magpies steal shiny objects to decorate their nests. We would miss them if gone and forgive their domination of the suet feeder, but make sure some is left for the little ones in cold weather.

Crow Clutch

Speaking of hawks, we have some local red-tailed. They will circle high looking for prairie dogs and western cottontails. Forest Service biologist and friend Cheron Ferland has used her professional skills at home on the west mesa to become a certified falconer. She captures a juvenile in the spring, often a threatened species, nurtures its development, trains it to hunt with her, then releases it back to the wild in fall. I wondered if this was exploitive domination but decided instead it is a human-wild partnership.

Last, the American crows are spirit guardians to some Native Americans, and maybe the rest of us if we attend. At times, we see a morning flock of two dozen having a grand time in our trees and corn patch. The Taos Land Trust Rio Fernando Park program has linked studies of their bird population to the land restoration work. Jim O'Donnell has described this extensively and reports in a recent *New Mexico* Magazine article that now some 190 bird species, two-thirds the number recorded in the whole country, can be found there. Priyanka Kumar, author and ornithologist who was a Leopold Writing

Program Mi Casita Resident in 2020, observed fifty-five species in Tres Piedras, at the edge of the Carson National Forest, twenty-six miles to the west during just the month of August.

Yes, there are ways to engage experiences with wild birds in our small places. I had a magnificent sighting one year while painting the Leopold cabin in October. Two large flocks of sandhill cranes flew south along the Tusas Mountains' ridge, heading to winter grounds at Bosque del Apache, and of course vigorously gobbling. Maybe they started from summer habitat in Sand County, Wisconsin. While steward of the human constructed Mi Casita, I try to have a biocentric grateful relationship with the wild cranes.

Loving the Rodents

Whether we are fostering habitat for them, or they have adapted to us, we live with various rodents. Starting small, the numerous deer mice find habitat and food in wood stacks, compost bins, straw piles, refuse bins, rock wall chinks. And they occasionally sneak into the house. Troi the dog conscientiously tells us when one is nocturnally nesting on the patio. Our sagebrush voles like to tunnel into mulched beds, especially beneath snowbanks, sometimes feasting on shrubbery roots. One year we grew potatoes in a bin of pig wire wrapped in quarter-inch hardware cloth, standing against the southwest corner of our fence, shaded by the blue spruce bosque. After several sprouts came up well, we noticed them disappearing. A little digging revealed vole tunnels coming through the open bottom. More hardware cloth there blocked them. Sorry critters, there's plenty else for you to eat.

Chipmunks are the next level foragers, especially in winter around the bird feeders when forest nourishment is scarce. We appreciate their contributions to the food chain, up and down. And they do excite our olfactory-astute dog around the wood pile.

Interesting rodent-human encounters occur at the Leopold cabin. The deer mice are intrusive, especially when they sense people using the kitchen. The Albuquerque-based Leopold Writing Program supports month-long residencies there for early to midcareer environmentalists. The twenty-one participants to date have been diverse in their wilderness/wildness experience. As free-range useful volunteer, one of my services is critter control. For some residents, the nocturnal sounds of mice in the ceiling spaces and the disposal task from traps have been unsettling adventures. And we need to be aware of Hanta virus exposure from mouse transmission. This is not quite what Leopold described as need for the wild, but it makes for interesting encounters nevertheless.

Returning to home, we have enclosed the west one third acre garden with four-feet high pig wire along the *latilla* fence, plus one-inch chicken wire on the bottom eighteen inches. This keeps out the many western cottontails that would devour our garden. However, both pocket gophers and prairie dogs have been on and within this land far longer than we have been; clearly, they intend to be here in the future. Cute as they may appear, however, prairie dogs do carry fleas, and rare cases of bubonic plague still occur. We've lost a few newly planted trees from their feasting on the roots. This challenges us to find peaceful coexistence methods.

The local old timers would drown them out with *acequia* flooding, or at least chase them to a distant field. We've accomplished that with plugging holes inside the fence and the dog's surveillance, but that has taken a few years. Needless to say, poisoning is indiscriminately toxic, to good predator hawks and owls as well. We are vigilant that our dog does not pick up a dead carcass. We have a few resident long-tailed weasels hunting the prairie dogs. One can set traps in gopher tunnels, but any victims are quickly replaced. When my west neighbor poisoned out his prairie dogs, pocket gophers quickly moved in.

I also tried the battery powered tubes that buzz every twenty-eight seconds, supposedly to scare them off. This tool was too artificial for effect. Ah, but this memoir is about experiences and strategies, not foolproof methods. When I was contributing native shrubs to the Leopold Cabin garden a few years ago and was concerned about abundant gopher mounds, Forest Service Biologist Bonnie told a story from her Bisbee, Arizona, childhood. She advised pounding a two-foot rebar into the mound half-way, then hanging an inverted plastic bottle so it rattles in the breeze. The random, naturalistic noise may spook the critters to go elsewhere. My results there and home seem to be 50 percent deterrence with this method.

Remember that we are discussing our wildness at home, but we are not at all isolated and remote. We can see dozens of houses on one half to full acre lots, with a few open fields and fallow areas between them. Striped skunks are seasonal visitors, particularly close to the border *acequias*. Our fence does exclude them, and we limit omnivore-attractive additions such as meats in the compost pile. We don't want our sweet dog to have a confrontation in the garden. But their nocturnal presence can be smelled some summer mornings. And many meet their end waddling too slowly across the road by nearby wetlands.

One mile north from our home, the Hondo Canyon and a Carson National Forest boundary begin. The road follows the Rio Hondo which flows out of the Taos Ski Valley peaks. We have watched the drama of human and North American beaver interaction along the river for decades. Dams have been blown up to allow water flow to farmlands downstream. Ponds have created breeding habitat for wild brown trout. Vacation cabins have been flooded. We learned much from the studies and experiences of Ben Goldfarb who completed writing his book *Eager, The Surprising Secret Life of Beavers and Why They Matter* when a Leopold Writing Program Resident.

Another intrusive wild creature is the common raccoon. They too usually just travel along the *acequias* that border the north and south ends of our half mile road, plus the *Acequia Madre* mother ditch running through the middle. They are uncanny in knowing when our corn has ripened and climb the fence at night to feast on a few choice ears. However, we have invoked help from a natural predator, spreading store-bought coyote urine granules outside the fence. That has limited the raccoons to just taking a tithe.

Predators Around Home

This brings us to the prevalent coyote, native to North America. The *Audubon Field Guide* includes the indigenous name "song dog." Judging by frequent howls and several often trotting in sight, there are three dens within a half mile. A breeding pair and a younger adolescent scout about in the morning within a few yards of our home, even down the open road. Spooky about people, they will change course, but with bravado. Not to be ignored, they leave scat piles in the road. We have seen them easily jump four-foot fences, but not ours. Troi the dog asserts her own territoriality often. I do not begrudge the coyotes their prairie dog meals. Tourist visitors are excited to hear the nocturnal songs, especially raucous when a successful hunt feast is brought to the den. We do warn about keeping small dogs on short leash and cats indoors, as a hunting pair may snatch them.

Besides entertainment value evoking Western atmosphere and trickster stories, how do we relate to them for Rewilding? They do have significant cultural identities. A few years ago, we often saw a skinny one with bare tail and patchy fur, unusually out in the midday sun. I learned in a Taos Master Gardener Program class that mangy coyotes were likely the source of the *Chupacabra* folklore, at least the *Norteño* version. This legendary canine-like creature acts strangely and supposedly drinks the blood of livestock, especially goats. Our mangy guy disappeared a year later. Unfortunately, it is not unusual to hear .22 shots from the El Salto old ranchito area. And poisoned bait is around; a friend lost his beloved Australian shepherd that way. The New Mexico Legislature just outlawed traps on public lands, due to both cruelty concerns and risks to people's dogs. Learn more from Dan Flores' 2016 *Coyote America: A Natural and Supernatural History.*

As we move our awareness of the wild to other predators, we have had a few sightings of stealthy bobcats, cousins of the lynx. We have learned to recognize their prints after a thin new snow. Since we are close to the Columbine-Hondo and Wheeler Peak Wilderness areas, black bears come visit, but they don't read Forest Service campground warning signs. Nor the ones we post on our neighborhood dumpster. Those are for the careless people.

Between abundant apple and native plum trees, our morning dog patrol discovers bear scat piles summer and fall, often right in the middle of our road. We once found bear scat on top of a neighbor's hot tub cover below overhanging chokecherry branches. They are shy and travel hidden among the trees along the *acequia* highways. We would not walk in the dark and risk surprising a sow with cub. And we also advise visitors and tourists to clean their fragrant barbecue grills and, in the fall, during prehibernation season when the bears are hungry, to take down their hummingbird feeders. Yes, there are more examples of how a Rewilding attitude finds ways to live in peaceful coexistence without human-caused damage.

Visiting Elk

Wild Grazing Herds

While our Philadelphia suburb adult kids consider wild deer as destructive pests, here we are happy to see them coming down from the National Forest. Occasionally, two or three mule deer will wander the open lanes between our fences. My neighbor next to the north end *acequia* woods frequently sees a buck with harem. We joke the guy seems stuck in a rut.

A half mile up the El Salto Peak foothills among the mixed conifers, people report wapiti elk. Down here, we just need to be careful driving at night. Friend Lewis Rosenthal has a home on three acres near the Weimar foothills of the Carson National Forest at the south end of town. The house and garden fill a fenced half acre, and the rest is open sage and grasses. He often sees elk browsing there, especially in the winter. I asked him what wildness attracts them, despite people's activity and cars on the road. He said the area used to be a ranch with unfenced grazing. The wild elk still consider it their habitat. Lewis is happy to see them. We compliment how he benefits from their contributions of fertilizer to his front garden.

Appreciating the Community

Here is a wonderful overview of midwinter's wild activity from a recent *National Wildlife* magazine. On the surface, the hawks, owls, coyotes, foxes, and weasels are hunting. Crows and ravens seek their usual carrion. Subnivean, under the snow, life is active. Some rodents are dormant in snow tunnels, while others occupy hibernation sanctuaries deeper in the soil. Our dog and I are fascinated to discover diverse tracks in the snow. While the critters themselves are seen less, the tracks tell many wild

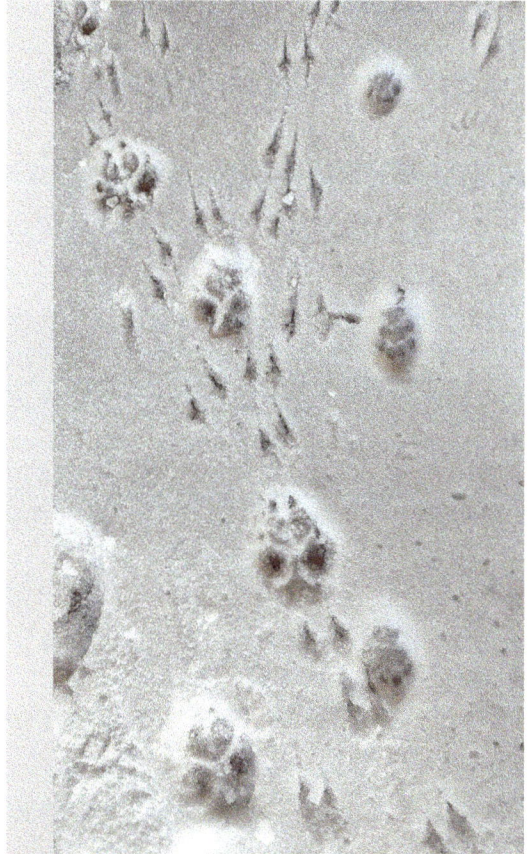

❖ Tracks in Snow

stories. They have their own ways, despite what humans impose.

Taos writer John Nichols' 1986 memoir *On the Mesa* captures his spiritual connection to a small wild place near Tres Orejas Peak that we can see from home:

On the mesa I collect nighthawk feathers, aerie bones, prairie dog and coyote skulls, Tres Orejas eagle feathers, a snakeskin from the Sheep Corral Overlook, the jawbones of pocket gophers and pocket mice, white-tipped sage thrasher tail feathers, owl pellets that include mouse skulls imbedded in their tightly packed fur, the iridescent breast feathers of waterfowl, and the hollow bodies of dung beetles and June bugs. Also a jackrabbit skull, a few small lichen stones, a graceful hunk of sheep vertebrae, and many sprigs of sage.

I take all these gimcracks home and keep them in a box. They are my big medicine bundle. When I travel, bits and pieces of the bundle travel with me. On airplanes, across continents, in strange hotels, I always carry the talismans of life on the quiet mesa. (Chapter 20).

✪ Sniffing for Critters

Wilder Homescape Food

5

There is value in any experience which reminds us of our dependency on the soil-plant-animal-man food chain.   Aldo Leopold, *Wildlife in American Culture,* 1941.

If we are seeking more wildness at home, our meals are paramount opportunities. Eating from our homegrown horticulture and husbandry sources contributes to this need. Yet in our small space and limited resources, we have to go beyond the home garden. One example is our current Homeowners' Association covenants that allow only "conventional pets." These rules exclude the free-range poultry we enjoyed at our 1970s Baja Corrales ranchito. We discuss human-imposed rules more in Chapter 6.

In our prior 2020 book, *Taos Horno Adventures: A Culinary Memoir Informed by History and Horticulture,* we told dozens of stories about events and recipes where the food was homegrown, locally sourced, and transformed by traditional beehive oven cooking. Yes, we can consider this a Rewilding practice, and therefore we introduce you to it now in this homescape book's context.

Rewilded eating rejects the anthropogenic, manufactured-by-humans foodscape. We can avoid the role Enrique Salman describes as *"Homo modernus industrialii."* Lisa Rayner distinguishes localvore from "invasivevore."

In his 2006 *The Omnivore's Dilemma,* Michael Pollan describes "the perfect meal." In his quest to expose and challenge the ignorance about food sources and their true cost, he plans a meal where he hunts, gathers, or grows all ingredients. They must be in season or fresh and represent diverse food groups such as animal, vegetable, mineral, and fungi. His personal goal was "would I learn anything of value about the nature and culture of human eating?" Mind you, he attempts this in the greater San Francisco Bay Area.

Well, the story of his many days foraging, cooking, then enjoying the multicourse sophisticated meal with friends is quite an odyssey. He comes to honor greater lines of relationship to source places and creatures eaten. Our view of his experience is recognizing the highly contrived and artificial characteristics of conventional domesticated foodscape and practices.

Group Sharing

One of our favorite culinary Rewilding experiences began when Forest Service Officer Ricardo Leon from Questa rewarded us with elk burger meat from his recent hunting harvest. Figuring how to use this treat with culinary adventurer friends, we decided to create an *horno* elk pizza. Annette provided her homegrown cherry tomatoes. Our Italian cooking school cheese consultant Marcie Coulter, spouse of my yeoman assistant cabin painter Darrell, chose Gruyère, mozzarella, and Parmesan. Cheron Ferland, Forest Service biologist, offered recently collected wild chanterelle mushrooms.

The crust then became my opportunity. I had recently propagated wild yeast sourdough starter from homegrown Pueblo blue corn flour. This became the crust. The pizza cooked on a stone in our outdoor *horno*, with cedar fire coals in an arc behind. Besides happy friendship and a glorious culinary experience, we felt gratified by the blend of localvore ingredients, authentic sourced provisions, and the opportunity to live some blended Taos cultural heritage.

✪ **Elk Pizza**

Sourdough Elk Pizza

Ingredients for a 12-inch crust

1 cup sourdough starter
1 ½ cups bread flour
½ cup warm water
1 tablespoon olive oil
½ teaspoon salt

1 Mix the sourdough starter, bread flour, warm water, olive oil, and salt.

2 Knead 10 minutes, then allow to rise in an oiled bowl for 1 hour at 70–80 degrees.

3 Knead again, then rest, cloth covered, for 10 minutes.

4 Flatten on a pizza pan covered with corn meal (preferably blue). Lift and pinch edges.

Ingredients for the toppings

2 cups sliced mushrooms
1 pound ground meat
1 cup cherry tomatoes
1 cup shredded mozzarella cheese
½ cup shredded Gruyère cheese
½ cup shredded Parmesan cheese
Italian seasoning mix

1 Sauté the 2 cups of mushrooms in a large skillet with olive oil. Set aside.

2 Brown the ground elk meat in the hot skillet. Set aside.

3 Slice 1 cup of cherry tomatoes. Set aside.

4 Combine the mozzarella, Gruyère, and Parmesan. Set aside.

5 Spread an additional 2 tablespoons olive oil on the crust. Add the browned elk, mushrooms, and tomatoes. Sprinkle on salt and Italian seasonings to taste. Spread the 3 cheeses on top. Dock the crust with a fork or roller.

6 Bake on the stone in the *horno*, monitoring and rotating, about 25 to 30 minutes, observing for good cheese melt but not edge char.

Our Historic Hearth

Our Horno

We regard our outdoor bee-hive-shaped brick oven, known locally by the Spanish name *horno*, as a wilder form of cooking. We call it Andalusian style as it blends Moorish and Iberian structure. It was designed and built by an Old Mexico crew. It consists of a concrete block base, volcanic stone heat sink interior, firebrick dome, clay stucco, and steel door. *Hornos* are also made from adobe bricks in New Mexico Pueblos and stacked stones in Middle Eastern communities. The heat comes from wood, locally sourced. The pots and tools are cast iron. The cooking experience outdoors engages us in a natural environment. The *horno* dynamics change in spring wind, summer heat, fall drizzle, and winter snow.

Even in the absence of industrial food processing, we can produce a variety of outcomes to preserve, dry, bake, roast, and fry. Smoke becomes a more complex entity, ranging from nuisance to fragrant atmosphere to agent of food transformation. Wood choice needs consideration, from kindling start to fire heat degree to burn duration, to flavor contributed. Last, *horno* cooking can transport our consciousness to our own ancestors and other cultures in myriad times and places when and where the wild was more intrinsic to daily life. See the 2020 *Taos Horno Adventures* book for many such stories and recipes.

Rewilding in Designated Wilderness

During our 1970s time living in Baja Corrales, we explored the Gila, Wheeler Peak, Pecos, and Jemez Wilderness Areas. Initial expeditions taught us that backpacks were too heavy, and our saddle horses were too skittish across streams. Bravo, the wildness spirits sent us a burro. A medium-sized grey jack with red ears and unknown age, we named him *Orejo Rojo*. This guy adjusted to wearing a pack saddle for gear bags. He even enjoyed riding in the pickup bed frame I built, at least after negotiating for a handful of sweet feed to get up the ramp.

With *Rojo's* help, we could carry a grill, skillet, and apple wood on trips. In those days, wild trout were plentiful in the Pecos. Our smoking method was simple. A light folding grill on the coals, apple wood to burn beneath, fish on the grill, and a wet burlap bag on top to hold the smoke.

As my fly fishing evolved to better conservation practices—I learned to release wild fish and avoid harassing the native cutthroats at all—I pursued graduates of the nearby Red River Hatchery. There are a few benefits to aging. At 65, one can fish the ponds at New Mexico Fish and Game hatcheries, as can kids under 12 and people with handicaps.

This privilege also accommodates for senior knees that discourage stream wading. And companion Troi, descendant of German water dog retrievers, loves to come along. The pond rules allow possession of three fish. This is the time when catch and release skills become handy—select the big ones and leave others for the kids with bait. The result: we often have rainbow trout in the freezer.

Our *horno* smoking method begins with a medium-sized fire.

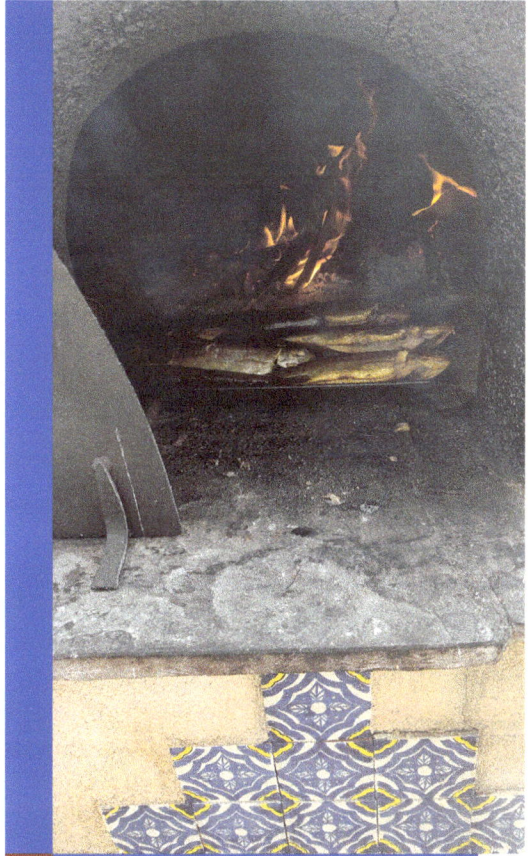

✦ **Trout Smoking**

I skip the usual kindling and like to use alder wood from the start. New Mexico alder, *Alnus oblongifolia,* grows along rivers and creeks. Various alder woods are traditional for fish smoking in the northern Midwest and Scotland. When not available, we have also smoked fish with apricot, plum, and apple woods sourced nearby.

Overnight brining with a coarse salt rub in the refrigerator firms the meat. However, soak the fish afterward at least an hour in fresh water to reduce the saltiness. Build a cedar fire and let it burn down to a hot coal bed in the *horno* rear. Add your smoking wood of choice, best if wetted. Then place the fish on a grill with legs in front of the fire; raising the grill allows heat and smoke to circulate all around. Plug the chimney hole and close the door. Expect much smoke; if it fades, open the door for more oxygen to reignite the fire. Periodic wood additions are usually needed. We have found small, nine to ten inch fish are good in one to two hours. Larger fifteen to sixteen inch fish may need two to three hours. One turnover is needed. If you go longer, you will have trout jerky. Not a bad idea either.

Now what do we make from this succulent smoked trout? Well, of course it is delicious straight, maybe with some melted butter as sauce. And here is the recipe we developed for Smoked Trout Schmear, which is great on sourdough bagels. Once again, see our *Horno Adventure* book for bagel mastery.

Smoked Trout Schmear

Ingredients
½ cup cream cheese
2 teaspoons Worcestershire sauce
4 tablespoons chopped chives, preferably from your garden
1 tablespoon capers
1 teaspoon salt
1 teaspoon lemon zest
2 tablespoons finely chopped celery
12 ounces of fish off the bones, about the yield from an average 15-incher or three 10-inchers
3 tablespoons sour cream

1 In a food processor, combine the cream cheese, Worcestershire, chives, capers, salt and zest. Process in short bursts until smooth. This can also be prepared without machinery in an old wooden mixing bowl, like the one Annette has from her grandmother.

2 Add the fish in small pieces until mixed but not mushy. Then thin with the sour cream. Add the celery.

3 Chill an hour before serving, but immediate tasting is allowed.

Wild Delicacy Beneath Our Feet

Wild Verdolagas in Our Corn Milpa

Many people believe common purslane, *Portulaca oleracea,* is an apparent weed in their gardens and lawns, an invasive from Europe. It is a low spreading succulent. I was pulling it from the vegetable beds and corn patch until Carmela Quinto introduced me to appreciation of the local *Norteño* recipe for *verdolagas*. Artist Anita Rodriguez in her 2016 *Coyota in the Kitchen* says *verdolagas* are "highly nutritious, pesticide free, high in Vitamin c and omega-3 fatty acids, and available outside the cash economy." Here is the recipe from Carmela's mother, Gloria in Pilar.

Verdolagas

Ingredients

A large bowlful of *verdolagas*, freshly picked the day you cook them. Cut the stems off the roots. They shrink when cooked.
Several scallions or wild green onions, *cebollín*
Bacon grease or cooking oil

1 Wash thoroughly, pat dry, chop to desired size.

2 Chop the onion.

3 Saute the mix until the *verdolagas* turn deep green. Serve warm or cold.

A distinctive and tangy taste! Carmela's boyfriend Felipe likes to add ground beef and green chile, Cordilera, New Mexico, style he says.

Working with the Tiny Wild

Another underappreciated wild friend of humans is yeast. The process of cultivating yeast to make leavened bread was discovered by the ancient Egyptians. Most modern commercial wheat flour is *Triticum aestivum,* developed in Persia, now Western Iran. This has the highest amounts of gluten components glutenin and gliadin that allow the dough to stretch without tearing, and therefore make lighter breads.

The popularity of leavened wheat bread spread from Egypt east to Mesopotamia and west to Greece. It followed the conquests of Alexander the Great, then the Romans through their extensive empire. The leavening yeast was kept alive as an active culture, what we now call sourdough starter.

The invention of commercial yeast in the nineteenth century shortened bread preparation time. However, in the American West, sourdough has had a mystique. Wagon trains, prairie settlers, and the California gold rush miners valued their starters, not having a dry goods store nearby for packaged yeast. It became common in San Francisco, even in 1968 when we explored California dreaming on holiday from work in Arizona. We enjoyed Dungeness crab and sourdough bread on Fisherman's Wharf. A sweet hippie girl even put flowers in Annette's hair.

So I was intrigued when Skip Belyea, a California refugee friend in Taos, encouraged me to bake sourdough in the new *horno*. After some research, making starter seemed feasible.

We realized this method was a way to engage the great biota by creating starter from the wild yeast living among us. Kiko Denzer describes catching the ambient yeast in one's kitchen for starter in his 2007 *Build your own Earth Oven*. After successfully creating a robust starter following standard recipes with commercial yeast, I decided to attempt it from the wild spores on our homegrown blue corn flour. Ah, a benefit of punting wash of the kernels, despite Annette's chagrin.

Blue Corn Wild Yeast Starter

1 In a 2-quart kitchen jar, mix 2 cups of warm water, 2 cups all-purpose flour, and 2 tablespoons of sugar.

2 Combine ½ cup homeground blue corn flour. Cover with a towel and let sit at 70-75 degrees.

3 As the wild yeast has less vigor than commercial hybrids, it is important to feed the starter daily with a cup of warm water and a cup of all-purpose flour. Then stir. Also, add another tablespoon of blue corn flour each day. You should see bubbling by 3-4 days and smell pungency.

4 By day 5, it is ready for use—having doubled in size if all has gone well. I named this colony Wild Blue.

Here's the recipe for Sourdough White Bread we bake in the outdoor *horno*. Our Wild Blue starter worked fine to make white flour bread.

Sourdough White Bread

Ingredients

1 cup sourdough starter
2 cups bread flour
½ cup warm water
Additional bread flour to firm when kneading
1 teaspoon salt

✸ **Horno Sourdough Bread**

1 Mix the bread flour and warm water with the sourdough starter.

2 Let rise overnight under moist cloth cover at room temperature.

3 Add ¼ cup flour and 1 teaspoon salt. Knead for 10 minutes, then rest it for 10 minutes under a moist cloth.

4 Transfer to a cloth covered oiled bowl and allow to rise about 3 hours at 75 to 80 degrees.

5 Sprinkle corn meal on the bottom of an 8-inch cast iron skillet or Dutch oven. Pour in the dough. Score the loaf top.

Heat the *horno* to about 350 degrees with a cedar fire in the rear. Rotate the skillet every 7 to 10 minutes to bake evenly. Keep the door closed to maintain heat. In about 30 minutes the crust will be light brown and a knife comes out clean. Annette likes when I minimize stray ash "campfire seasoning."

Thinking about cornbread, we wondered if our wild yeast starter would work. Traditional cornbread uses baking powder, a commercial chemical mixture, for leavening. Using the usual half corn meal and half wheat flour mix, the result was heavier, likely from less gas production. But the experience was wilder!

After leaving New Mexico for Wisconsin, Aldo Leopold's family spent much time at their "Shack" on eighty acres of depleted Sand County farmland. As they lived simply in relationship with wildness, here's the recipe for Leopold Family Sourdough Pancakes, reproduced as provided verbatim by Laura at the Baraboo, Wisconsin, Aldo Leopold Foundation Archives.

Leopold Family Sourdough Pancakes

Ingredients

½ cup sourdough starter
1 cup warm water
1 cup flour
1 egg
1 teaspoon baking soda
2 tablespoons sugar
½ teaspoon salt

The night before: Mix 1 cup of flour, ½ cup warm water, and ½ cup starter. Take it to bed with you to keep it warm.

In the morning: Add 1 egg, 1 teaspoon of baking soda, 2 tablespoons of sugar, and ½ teaspoon of salt. Lightly whisk just to mix. Let it sit twenty minutes. Grease and preheat a ten-inch skillet. Use about ¼ cup of batter to make an eight-inch pancake. Pour in the batter and roll around the pan so it is thin. When the bubbles have popped and the top is dry, flip it over. Makes eight to ten pancakes.

To serve: add butter and put bacon, sausage, or cinnamon sugar on top. Roll up the pancake. Add maple syrup. Enjoy!

Rewilding with Fowl

Come the Fourth of July, we pursued a plan to smoke a turkey in the *horno*. Traditional locals have several methods for this, often with "falling off the bone" reports. One irony is the small brown wild turkey of New England that we observed around Northern Vermont, now abundant after control of excessive hunting, is not the typical commercial large white bird. That species is native to South

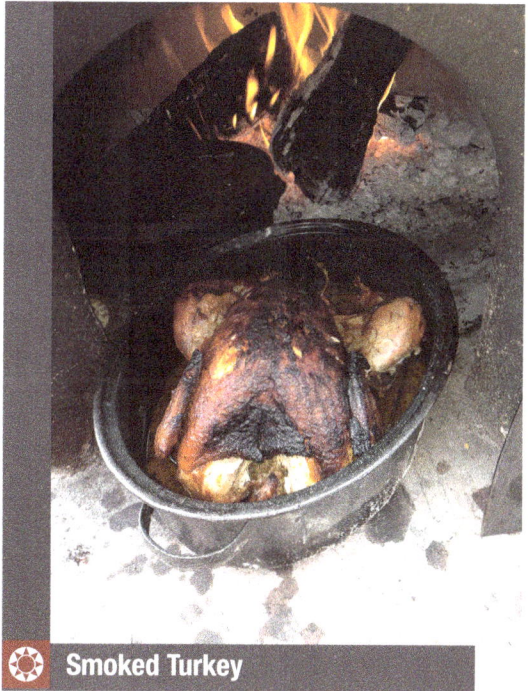

✪ Smoked Turkey

America and was domesticated by the Aztecs who made elegant clothing from the feathers woven with cotton. Cortez brought specimens to Europe, and it was later introduced back to colonial North American farming. There is also evidence of turkeys traded from Mesoamerica to ancient cultures in the southwest. Therefore, this becomes an experience of traditional culinary Rewilding.

Researching woods for smoking, and also seeking one locally sourced, I found confirmation that heavier smoke flavors such as oak, hickory, mesquite, and cedar should be avoided with fowl. In general, fruitwoods are preferred. Eureka! The large fallow field south of our home has dozens of old plum trees. Wild plums grow profusely in the ditches along Arroyo Seco roads, usually as shrubs, and can become small trees. The most common variety is a native according to Carter, *Prunus americana.* However, records of the early seventeenth century Franciscan missions, as at Santa Fe, indicate European varieties were brought and established here, including "very good plums" according to Dunmire's 2004 *Gardens of New Spain.* Our *Norteño* informants agree that the introduced fruit are usually larger than the two-centimeter size natives. The native plums should not be confused with *Prunus virginiana* and *Prunus serotina,* common choke cherry and southwestern black cherry.

Plum Wood Smoked Turkey

Ingredients
A 12- to 14- pound turkey
1 cup sea salt
1 cup brown sugar or maple syrup
12 fresh thyme sprigs
5 bay leaves

1 Brine the turkey in a large roasting pan with sea salt, sugar or syrup, thyme sprigs, and bay leaves dissolved in enough water to cover. Refrigerate for 24 hours. Soak the dry plum wood.

2 Build a moderately sized fire of kindling wood in the *horno* rear and let it burn down to a bed of coals. Then put on pieces of the wetted fruit wood to begin the smoking.

3 Wash the brine off the bird, soak in fresh water 30 minutes, and place in a roasting pan, lid off. Close the smoke hole and adjust the *horno* door to allow sufficient air for wood smoking without flaming.

4 Rotate and turn over the bird in the roasting pan about every half hour. Regulate the door air intake to allow some flame for maintaining the coals, but usually keep the door closed for intense smoke. Be prepared to add more dampened smoking wood as needed.

5 We use a small dial oven thermometer standing inside the *horno* to monitor the temperature. It should be about 200 degrees. Basting with pan drippings will keep the bird moist.

6 At about 4 hours, probe the breast or thigh joint for juiciness. Try to keep the coals glowing so you can continue to smoke slowly.

From Ancient Story to Rewilded Truth

We will end with a historic story about human food in a wilderness that was elevated to sacred status. You are familiar with the Old Testament story of the manna that nourished the

Israelites after their Exodus from Egypt. They attributed its appearance to a divine miracle. It turns out that the manna is a carbohydrate secretion of aphids that live on acacia trees. Think of it like bees making honey. It is produced nocturnally, then evaporates during the day. One needs to know how and when to find it. Modern desert-dwelling Bedouins still harvest manna. Is this a miracle, or just humans attentive to wild gifts from Nature? Maybe that question is what makes the gifts sacred.

✪ Horno Gratitude

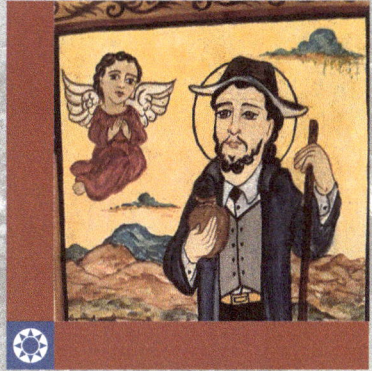

Contemplative Rewilding

6 ✦

That land is a community is the basic concept of ecology, but that land is to be loved and respected is an extension of ethics. Aldo Leopold, *The Ecological Conscience,* 1947.

I learned about the application of contemplative methods to ecology from Professor Paul Wapner. Over several years, he has conducted a retreat at the Lama Foundation in northern New Mexico on Contemplative Environmental Practices. Lama is an interspiritual, intentional community that has provided teaching of world religions in an alternative rural mountain setting since 1968. Ecological adaptations and permaculture cultivation methods are fundamental practices. I attended the five-day retreat event for two consecutive years.

While Buddhism is among the observances, most famously from the teaching there by Ram Dass, the name *Lama* comes from "moss" in the old Spanish dialect of northern New Mexico, according to Ruben Cobos's 1983 *Dictionary of New*

Mexico and Southern Colorado Spanish. At 8,000 feet, the conifer forest and meadow lands are high in moisture from summer monsoons and winter snows. In Chapter 2, we wrote about the Lama water spring and vigorous aspen growth. However, fitting the ambiance more, T.M. Pearce's 1965 *New Mexico Place Names: A Geographical Dictionary* defines *Lama* as meaning "mud."

How can we understand *contemplative* as valuable to the action world of ecological preservation and restoration initiatives, and particularly to the strategy of Rewilding? Thus far, we have described personal practices in our small homescape for ecosystem preservation and more than human enhancement. We do use beneficial environmental technology, such as solar electric panels, reduction in fossil fuel use, and passive solar heating. We also have fireplaces, insulation, a wood burning *horno* instead of the gas stove, reduced energy consumption lighting, selectiveness in sourcing commercial food, avoidance of toxic domestic products, and various recycling efforts.

Views of The Process

Contemplative methods emphasize observation and thought, rather than action. While certain religions call their prayer contemplative, the approach also includes formal meditative techniques. Additional contemplative qualities may be described as pensive, musing, ruminative, and reflective. Therefore, we add these forms to our human motivation that leads to practices.

We think the most powerful benefit of contemplative practices is fostering moral sensitivity to the consequences of human actions. One way to resolve Leopold's appeal to live in community, not commodify and dominate Nature, is to seek identity there. We are the same in many ways, all part of Nature. At one of the Lama Contemplative Retreats, I learned this song by Buddhist Teacher Thich Nhat Hanh:

> And when I rise, let me rise, Like a bird, joyfully.
> And when I fall, let me fall, Like a leaf, gracefully, without regret.
> And when I stand, let me stand, Like a tree, strong and tall.
> And when I lie, let me lie, Like a lake, peacefully, calm and still.
> And when I work, let me work, Like a bee, wholeheartedly.
> And when I play, let me play, Like a breeze, fresh and cool, light and clear.

Have we strayed too far into the spiritual? We see similarity to choosing actions in our small place with the guidance given by Parker Palmer in his 1999 *Let Your Life Speak.* When deciding to speak in a Quaker service, and in life, consider:

> Is it true? Is it good? Is it necessary?

This wisdom came to us from longtime friend Lawrence Cook. When he taught elementary school reading in Albuquerque, a parent compared him to Mr. Rogers. We see this interpersonal ethical pragmatism as applicable to actions in our ecosphere community. Adding humility to stewardship makes the whole larger than any anthropogenic self.

The Importance of Place

This is where the power of place requires our awareness. Numerous environmental writers and philosophers have studied and discussed the importance of place. We will limit attention to our immediate experience of land and culture here in the Taos area, as a continuation of the historical wandering described in Chapter 1. We consider place as a process, not just an object. Friend Lawrence has a retreat adjacent to the South San Juan Wilderness. He blesses a sprout emerging from an old Douglas fir stump as "Little Tree," a beloved childrens' story.

We have learned the *Norteño* version of walkabout, called *paseando*. Troi, the dog, makes a sniffing circuit of our garden perimeter fence dutifully first thing every morning. Occasionally, a young prairie dog or cottontail bunny has squeezed through but gets very surprised. Troi's temperament is not to kill them, but she barks persistently to alert me. I toss them over the fence with a shovel into the neighbor's weedy field. Later in the morning, after coffee, I make the same circuit. As my nature is more visual than olfactory, I greet the trees, monitor the compost piles, scout for plant signs of the season, and observe for secretive creatures. And as guided by Paul Kingsnorth, I look for what our small natural place might need from us. Then we take a walk around outside the fence to check more trees there, look for new gopher mounds closing in, and assess the weeds, seeking the day's measure of balance.

We are reminded of a *paseando* prayer from our own ancestors' culture. Hasidic Rebbe Nachman of Breslov, Poland, taught this in about 1800. Unity music director Jenny Bird transformed it for her 2015 *Sage Songs* album.

> May it be my custom to go outdoors each day among the trees and grasses, among all growing things, there to be alone and enter into prayer. There may I express all that is in my heart, talking with the Creator to whom I belong.

> And may all grasses, trees, and plants awake at my coming and send the power of their life into my prayer, making whole my heart and my speech through the life and spirit of growing things, made whole by their transcendent Source.

Remembering the original literal meaning of Wildness, the Rabbi's practices seem to qualify as regard for autonomy and self-will. As we bring in more spiritual aspects to this narrative, let us distinguish it from philosophical writing with abstract, idealistic, artful goals. To reiterate the Introduction, our story is about current practicality, effectiveness, and pedestrian actions. I compare my old school's burning in wartime to environmental destruction. Appreciating the rebuilding by the Freemasons, I still follow their inspirational motto "Toward a widening sphere of usefulness." This seems "true, good, and necessary."

Personal Measures of Rewilding

We emphasize the contemplative characteristic of thoughtfulness. Annette offered a concept from her work with gifted education: metacognition. This means the process of thinking about thinking. While drafting these stories about Rewilding in our home environment, we realized that Rewilding strategic efforts and outcomes can occur in a wide range of degrees. And should.

More than a joke, we like the wisdom that 50 percent of something is better than 100 percent of nothing. Maybe my work as a physician attunes us; health improvement outcomes are often measured in degrees, not absolutes. Maybe we are also influenced by being the parents of a son with lifelong developmental disabilities. We also performed much devoted work as adaptive ski instructors of people with disabilities where small increments of progress are welcome and joyful.

We thought about how this was expressed in our home horticulture and husbandry. I considered the twelve Austrian pines we planted. On the one hand, we can judge them as not wild, but rather exotic imports. However, they are botanically very similar to the prevalent native ponderosa pines. These Austrians have been thriving with us for several years. The larger and older trees are established and self-sufficient, needing less from us, such as watering and mulching. So how are we to evaluate their degree of wildness? 50, 75, 95 percent? This thinking process leads me again to the concept of **wilder**ness as our goal; there is a spectrum of wild possible.

How much does relative wild exist with any of our ecosphere companions? And how much can the degree of wild in them be preserved, restored, and regenerated? Let's parse these qualities. First, we can practice Rewilding by preserving what exists. Yet we are going to confront the common dualism that sees wild as different from human, as something separate, "out there." We are all still wild in some ways, to some degree.

Secondly, we can restore some wildness that has been lost from all dimensions of the ecosphere. Thirdly, we can revitalize diminished wild processes through regeneration, helping them become autonomous again. And we propose a fourth, called progressive conversion of the unwilded back to wild. In your daily home walkabout, observe for artificial and industrial entities where humans have removed the wildness. Ask if they can be made wild again in new ways. This is in the spirit of Paul Wapner's concept "brave new wildness." We can model after Leopold when he states:

> There are some who can live without wild things, and some who cannot.

We appeal for practicing our own wildness among all things in life.

Wild is not Chaotic

Coming back to considering a wilder human role in our homescape, we observe that wild does not necessarily mean chaotic. Yes, the popular appeal for stewardship is important, but that is still tied to attitudes of human presumption and ownership. And yes, we are back to Leopold's calling out the Abrahamic dominion concepts. What then can we do to practice a Rewilding strategy with land ownership methods in our current society? Can private property rights be compatible with Rewilding strategies? From a contemplative perspective, how can we think about ownership that is not anthropocentric? While we distinguish stewardship from relationship in community with all that is natural, we believe certain human social systems can foster wildness qualities. Terry Tempest Williams has called for an ecological "community of care."

Let's think about various legal structures for land ownership. We focus here on individuals or small groups in current society, not governments, sovereign Native tribes, or historic tenancy, like the colonial New Spain *encomienda* system. In our current democracy, if you are fortunate to legally own land, no matter how small, property rights are protected by civil law. If one is renting, you have a lease structure. Additional salutary levels of influence may be applied, such as deed restrictions, covenants, and local ordinances.

For example, our Homeowners Association only allows "conventional pets," preventing wilder and natural attributes we could have with more than human companions. Back in the 1970s, we lived in a rural Baja Corrales neighborhood without restrictions. This allowed us to share our three quarters of an acre with two horses, a burro, chickens, turkeys, and ducks, besides the dog and barn cats. We surely enjoyed and learned from this diverse community. And that jack burro *Rojo* was quite a character, braying at dawn like the roosters.

Native plant enthusiasts criticize HOAs that require conventional lawns with their typical toxins and rules that punish wilder foodscapes, fields of wildflowers, or un-cut native prairie grasses. Covenants and ordinances can be changed to promote small place wildness. Many organiza-tions provide such guidance.

Moving to consider individual ownership legal systems, we have our home in a Family Revocable Trust. Commonly done for estate tax advantages and inheritance efficiency, a trust can establish standards for the use and care of the land. Revo-cable Trusts are also simple to prepare and amend. We have stipulated who will inherit the homescape and what resources will sustain it. While not ironclad in authority, this vehicle at least makes our intentions clear and fosters continuity of the wildness qualities.

Rewilding beyond your Homescape

The next preservation level is establishment of a Conserva-tion Easement through a Land Trust, as that in Taos. While usually reserved for larger land spaces than our homescape, the concept is very appealing for our Rewilding purposes, be-yond the depreciation-based financial tax advantages. Usual-ly, an important land quality is required such as scenic, eco-logical, or historic value to qualify as an easement. Small places may be more difficult to have accepted by an admin-istering agency. However, if approved, such an arrangement can be an ongoing Rewilding, Preservation, and Conservation strategy.

We recognize the Taos Land Trust as a comprehensive local resource for our horticulture and husbandry interests. Through their Rio Fernando Park Restoration site, native plant and or-ganic gardening demonstrations are valuable. They link local bird watching studies with their ecological programs. We see in their programs attempts to use more traditional and natural water management, less dependent on "nonwild" technology.

Yes, as with rejuvenating our old grazing field homescape, a wilder community park initiative can bring beneficence.

The Taos Land Trust purchased twenty acres of neglected farmland close to town several years ago. It has recently been certified as a Conservation Easement under the Santa Fe Land Trust's supervision. The Rio Fernando running through is now a naturalized water course with wetlands. Native vegetation has been planted and beavers have returned. A dry *acequia* has been restored to water the organic demonstration garden. Several acres of weeds have been replanted with restorative cover crops. Invasive Siberian elm trees have been pruned back and Russian olives uprooted to allow native tree growth. The staff have organized community support programs such as a Healthy Soil Initiative in conjunction with the Taos Valley Acequia Association *parciante* users. In addition, home food growing boxes are being distributed to families in need during our pandemic. An ingenious Pollinator Concentrator garden and sculpture have been installed, featuring a base of figurative tiles made by local school children. It is now a public park for all people to experience, accessible in their town.

We will end describing the Taos Land Trust with this history recorded by James Bull in his 1998 *Out of Time* book. The Trust was established in 1991, in part due to the gift by author Frank Waters and his wife Barbara of their Arroyo Seco land as the first Conservation Easement. In his founding letter to the Trust, Waters stated:

> We are not the owners of the land we occupy, nor its tenants, nor simply its caretakers. We are a part of the living earth itself.

Personal Practice Opportunities

We would like to leave you with ideas to practice beyond your small homescape. Some of our language may seem common and simplistic. But as truths are often repeated, we fear no clichés.

We described our Taos Land Trust. If not having land to conserve with your local organization, volunteer in their programs. Easements need monitoring for ongoing compliance and management. Volunteering to be a monitor, I was rewarded with assignment to the Frank Waters Family Trust Easement which is nearby our home up the El Salto foothills. There will be more to learn from this evolving experience.

Consider opportunities for educational programs, from farmers to home gardeners to schoolkids. Demonstration gardens can be informative and sources of community food provision. Identify organizations that practice restoration and preservation on public lands near you.

When Leopold was limited to a desk job after his illness, he founded the Albuquerque Wildlife Federation in 1924. The current group is robust at work on public land many week-

✿ Mi Casita Historic Site

ends. They even helped paint the Mi Casita cabin last year and joined in the installation of a National Historic Site plaque.

Seek spiritual inspiration from your own community's cultures. Our Taos Buddhist Hanuman Temple developed permaculture systems for their ritual feast observances. New Mexico Catholics honor San Ysidro, the patron of farmers. A nearby village is named for him and images decorate church retablo altar screens. We enjoy a modern interpretation piece on our dining room wall. He is holding a small bag of grain which represents one year of his meager crop. But when traveling to the mill for its grinding, he came upon a flock of

✳ San Ysidro Retablo

hungry birds. He generously fed them some seed. When he arrived at the mill, his grain had miraculously doubled in amount.

In our ancient Hebrew history, I regard the booths of *Sukkot* as the temporary shelters where the pastoral people lived while harvesting their fields. Partially open to the sky, a *sukkah* encourages connection to the universe. The entire family joined in the devoted work and gratitude for the harvest.

Adding to possible practices, others have written extensively about community food gardens, especially in urban settings. Contribute to these efforts for everyone's nurture. My friend Lawrence shared the observation of Quaker Parker Palmer that humus and humility have the same Latin root, low of the earth. Instead of just observer attitudes, we are moving toward encouragement of self-awareness that people are nature and nature is in our humanity. That seems to me truly community kinship. This is not obscure to us, an old physician and nurturing teacher.

Indulge us in sharing a story you may find useful to engage with a Rewilding immersion experience. I have described my connection with the legacy of Aldo Leopold through volunteering for the US Forest Service. This did not happen because I am special. It was a combination of fortunate opportunity and adaptive usefulness. Joining the Taos chapter of the New Mexico Native Plant Society on retiring, the Board leaders asked me to help arrange field trips, knowing I had done much exploring here. Scouting around for guides, I located Forest Service staff Bonnie Woods based at the Tres Piedras station. She led our group on field trips to the Stewart Meadows and Valle Vidal Preserves.

A few months later, I received a call asking for help with a project at the Leopold cabin. One of the Leopold Writing

Program Residents was Bonnie Harper Lore, a botanist from Minnesota who consulted with state highway departments on developing native plantings. She proposed we establish a native plant demonstration garden at the cabin. After receiving Forest Service administrative approval and archaeologic survey clearance, Bonnie Woods asked me for practical help. We shopped for some forbs and shrubs as available, then shared planting tasks. These included community events of seeding and mulching, once with a kids' group. And yes, I have since made dozens of visits for watering and gopher interventions. We also lucked into some plant identification signs, left over from a Native Plant Society community grant project.

I worked with several Forest Service professionals, including "holding the fort" duty when staff changed assignments. In the midst of intense national conflict over the Trump administration's adverse environmental policies, I learned to respect the devoted local staff attempting to do the best they could, despite the politics at higher levels. Aldo Leopold's first duty as Carson Supervisor was developing a grazing permit system just a few years after the National Forests were established. Open land regulations were not welcome during two hundred years among *Norteño* sheep herders and one hundred years of *Tejano/Anglo* cattle ranchers. One result of Leopold's engagement with this issue was his realizing the importance of the food chain in maintaining a healthy ecosystem. In addition to restricting overgrazing, his efforts led to new wildlife conservation advocacy.

A funny and credible anecdote occurs in John Nichol's *Milagro Beanfield War* novel and movie, set sometime in the 1970s. Despite also being *Norteño*, the Forest Service Ranger character is disliked by the other locals, particularly when he is a stooge for the Anglo developers' golf course scheme. When the hero Joe Mondragon's cow was lured onto Forest

Service land as harassment, the smart sheriff Bernie refused to make an arrest because the cow did not eat any government grass.

Wherever your location, opportunities to Rewild can be found with an attitude of attentiveness. The Aldo Leopold Foundation in Baraboo, Wisconsin, publishes an annual calendar of regional Phenology. This is defined as the study of cyclic and seasonal natural phenomena, especially in relation to climate, plant, and animal life. Leopold pursued this actively at the Shack. While our northern New Mexico homescape is far from Sand County, the calendar data and stories are very engaging.

Our practice messages: build relationship with your homescape, listen for needs, follow directions from the wildness, build on what flourishes, and be generous with community needs. Annette explained recently to a Taos gardener friend,

> Yes, in the big picture things can be sad and frustrating and disheartening, but we do what we can to make positive change in our small home sphere of influence.

We have both carried for decades the spirit of this traditional Shaker hymn, "Simple Gifts."

> 'Tis the gift to be simple, 'tis the gift to be free.
> 'Tis the gift to come down where you ought to be.
> And when we find ourselves in the place just right,
> 'Twill be in the valley of love and delight.
>
> When true simplicity is gained,
> To bow and to bend we shan't be ashamed.
> To turn, turn will be our delight,
> Till by turning, turning we come round right.

References

Abram David. *The Spell of the Sensuous.* Vintage Books, 1997.

Alden, Peter and Peter Friederici. *National Audubon Society Field Guide to the Southwestern States.* Alfred Knopf Inc, 1999.

Bernstein, Ellen. *Ecology and the Jewish Spirit: Where Nature and the Sacred Meet.* Jewish Lights Publishing, 2000.

Berry, Wendell. *Think Little.* Counterpoint, 2019.

Bird, Jenny. "Holy Tree," by permission. In *Songs of Trees,* 2001. Jennybird.com

Bull, James C. *Out of Time, Arroyo Seco: An Historic Look at a 250 Year Old Northern New Mexico Village.* Wolff Publishing Works, 1998.

Burney, Michael et al. "Archaeological and Historical Survey of Three Acres South of the Millicent Rogers Museum," El Prado, by permission. Unpublished, 2019.

Cobos, Ruben. *A Dictionary of New Mexico and Southern Colorado Spanish.* Museum of New Mexico Press, 1983.

Coles, Robert. *The Old Ones of New Mexico.* University of New Mexico Press, 1973.

deBuys, William and Alex Harris. *River of Traps: A Village Life.* University of New Mexico Press, 1990.

Denzer, Kiko. *Build Your Own Earth Oven.* Hand Print Press, 2007.

Dunmire, William. *Gardens of New Spain: How Mediterranean Plants and Foods Changed America.* University of Texas Press, 2004.

Feiler, Bruce. *Abraham: A Journey to the Heart of Three Faiths.* William Morrow, 2002.

Flores, Dan. *Coyote America: A Natural and Supernatural History.* Basic Books, 2016.

Goldfarb, Ben. *Eager: The Surprising, Secret Life of Beavers and Why They Matter.* Chelsea Green, 2018.

Ivey, Robert DeWitt. *Flowering Plants of New Mexico,* 4th ed. Ivey Publishers, 2003.

Joslin, Les, ed. *Walt Perry: An Early Day Forest Ranger in New Mexico and Oregon.* Wilderness Associates, 1999.

Kingsnorth, Paul. *Confessions of a Recovering Environmentalist and Other Essays.* Graywolf Press, 2017.

Leopold, Aldo. *A Sand County Almanac.* Oxford University Press, 1949.

Lowenfels, Jeff and Wayne Lewis. *Teaming With Microbes: The Organic Gardener's Guide to the Soil Food Web.* Rev. ed. Timber Press, 2010.

Meine, Kurt. *Aldo Leopold: His Life and Work.* University of Wisconsin Press, 1988.

Middleton, Natalie. *Orion: People and Nature,* Spring 2021, p.60.

New Mexico State College of Agriculture, Consumer, and Environmental Sciences. *Troublesome Weeds of New Mexico.* Las Cruces, 2010.

Nichols, John. *On the Mesa.* Ancient City Press, 1986.

—— *If Mountains Die: A New Mexico Memoir.* W.W. Norton, 1979.

Pearce, T. M., ed. *New Mexico Place Names: A Geographical Dictionary.* University of New Mexico Press, 1965.

Plotica, Luke. "Politics is not enough: Individual action and the limits of institutions," in *The Ecological Citizen,* Vol. 4 No. 1, 2020.

Prestwood, Hugh. "Bristlecone Pine." by permission. Hughprestwood.com.

Rayner, Lisa. *Growing Food in the Southwest Mountains: A Guide to High Altitude, Semi-Arid Home Permaculture Gardens,* 4th ed. Lifeweaver, 2013.

Rodriguez, Anita. *Coyota in the Kitchen: A Memoir of New and Old Mexico.* University of New Mexico Press, 2016.

Rubin, Richard and Annette. *Taos Horno Adventures: A Multicultural Culinary Memoir Informed by History and Horticulture.* Nighthawk Press, 2020.

Safina, Carl. *Becoming Wild.* Henry Holt, 2020.

"Simple Gifts." Traditional Shaker Hymn. From the Unity of Taos Songbook, by permission.

Starr, Mirabai. *God of Love: A Guide to the Heart of Judaism, Christianity, and Islam.* Monkfish Company, 2012.

—— *Wild Mercy: Living the Fierce and Tender Wisdom of the Women Mystics.* Sounds True, 2019.

Stuart, David E. *Anasazi America,* 2nd ed. University of New Mexico Press, 2014.

Tallamy, Douglas W. *Nature's Best Hope: A New Approach to Conservation That Starts in Your Yard.* Timber Press, 2019.

Tapia, Steve. *Oikos: Ecology of Northern New Mexico.* Nighthawk Press, 2016.

Van Horn, Gavin and John Hausdoerffer. *Wildness: Relations of People and Place.* University of Chicago Press, 2017.

Wapner, Paul. *Is Wildness Over?* Polity Press, 2020.

Wasowski, Sally. *Native Gardening in Northern New Mexico.* Native Plant Society of New Mexico, 2003.

Waters, Frank. *People of the Valley.* Swallow Press, 1941.

Winkler, Gershon. *Ceremony for the Ancient Hebraic Mid-Winter Festival of Trees.* Walking Stick Foundation, 2021.

Wohlleben, Peter. *The Hidden Life of Trees: What They Feel, How They Communicate—Discoveries from A Secret World.* Greystone Books, 2015

Useful Topic Index

⊛ AUTHORS AND ARTISTS

✪ DEFINITIONS

✪ FAUNA

✹ RESOURCES AND TEACHERS

Richard's lifelong descriptive writing began with a college dual major in English and Biology, and a medical career ranging from Southwestern community health initiatives to Developmental Disability practice, teaching, and research. Annette's career began with a Psychology major, then progressed to degrees in School Counseling, Elementary Education, Special Education, and Gifted Education. Beyond their professions, the authors describe their meaningful life experiences with ecological values in this book's stories.

This book is a sequel to our works of craft, community, and philanthropy.

www.ingramcontent.com/pod-product-compliance
Lightning Source LLC
Chambersburg PA
CBHW041220030426

42336CB00024B/3407